KWIK·SEW®
METHOD FOR
EASY SEWING

by Kerstin Martensson

First Printing, September 1980
Second Printing, March 1981
Copyright 1980 by Kerstin Martensson
All rights reserved. No part of this may be reproduced in any form
or by any process, without permission in writing from copyright owner.
Printed in the United States of America
ISBN 0–913212–09–1

about the author

 KWIK·SEW METHOD FOR SEWING KNIT AND STRETCH FABRIC was the first book on home sewing by Kerstin Martensson. It was first published in 1968. This is the third revision to cover the more up-to-date sewing techniques and the latest knit and stretch fabrics now available. Kerstin has written eleven books on home sewing, six of which are still published. The overwhelming acceptance of Kerstin Martensson's books can be attributed to their illustrated, easy-to-follow, step-by-step procedures.

Over a million copies of her books have been sold thus far. Many of these are being used by schools and colleges throughout the western world as sewing textbooks.

Kerstin Martensson is the President of KWIK·SEW Pattern Co., Inc. and is internationally known as one of the foremost home economists. Kerstin was born in Gothenberg, Sweden and educated in both Sweden and England. She specialized in clothing construction, pattern design and fashion and heads the Design Department of KWIK·SEW Pattern Co., Inc. She has conducted training classes in all phases of sewing in the United States and Canada, as well as England, Germany and the Scandinavian countries.

Kerstin's distinguished career as author, designer and lecturer includes numerous television and radio appearances. She also has been credited with making the first film dealing exclusively with the techniques of sewing stretch fabrics at home. Her latest three films entitled "Anyone Can Sew Knit and Stretch Fabrics" have been extremely well received in the United States and Canada.

All of Kerstin Martensson's books are carefully revised prior to each printing to keep them updated in the latest and newest sewing techniques. Other books now available are:

SEW FOR BABY - THE FUN WAY
SEW FOR TODDLERS
PROFESSIONAL PATTERN ALTERATIONS MADE EASY
KWIK·SEW METHOD FOR SEWING MEN'S WEAR
KWIK·SEW METHOD FOR SEWING LINGERIE

BOARD OF DIRECTORS

KWIK-SEW Pattern Co., Inc.

introduction

If you ever have an opportunity to look at an old pattern, you can sometimes find them in stores featuring old books or occasionally in an antique store, you will be amazed at how complicated they used to be. There were literally dozens of pieces all necessary to construct the very complicated dresses with their ruffles, puffed sleeves, fancy laces and trim. There was also a tremendous amount of tailoring and hand sewing which was needed to construct one garment. In addition, you have to remember that a sewing machine could only sew a straight stitch; it was the unusual sewing machine that could sew in reverse and the great majority were powered by use of a treadle or were hand cranked.

Because sewing was so complicated only a few women had the necessary skills to produce a garment which did not look home made. In addition, doing your own sewing was considered to be of very "low status".

The revolution in home sewing has been brought about because of a number of factors. One of the most important ones was the increased cost of finished garments. As the "sweat shops" were unionized, many manufacturers fled the industrial areas in search of cheaper labor, the union organizers followed them and eventually the entire garment industry became one of the most highly unionized industries in the country.

Immediately following World War II, the American government lowered the import duty on sewing machines in order to assist the various European countries rebuild their economies. Zigzag sewing machines were introduced, followed by automatic zigzag machines, and finally by the sophisticated reverse cycle machines available today. Now, a woman can, on her home machine perform the complicated sewing stitches formerly found only on commercial machines.

About the same time as the new sewing machines became available, a tremendous breakthrough occurred in the fabric business. Synthetic fabrics of all kinds and descriptions began to be found in fabric stores. This gave a tremendous boost to home sewing, for now stretch fabric was available to the home sewer.

These stretch fabrics, coupled with simplified patterns, made it possible for even a beginning sewer to turn out professional looking garments. Then along came stretch thread which made the home sewer's task even easier.

These new techniques are especially appreciated by women who can devote only a limited time for home sewing. You can construct an almost limitless number of different garments using knit and stretch fabrics. These could include tops, slacks, swimwear, dresses, suits, etc. Almost daily, new improved fabrics appear on the market. Regardless of the type of knit and stretch fabric the same basic rules apply on how to sew them.

contents

general
sewing
information

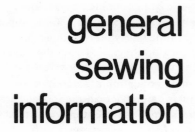

Knitted fabrics possess "stretch" because of the way they are constructed. There are three basic types of knitted fabric; sweater knit, single knit and double knit.

Single knit is knitted on a machine which uses one row of needles. The face is smooth and has lengthwise vertical rows; the back has horizontal rows (of half circles purl knit). Single knits stretch more in width than in length and usually have a moderate stretch, about 18%. Single knit fabric can be used for T-shirts, blouses, and dresses.

Double knit is knitted on a machine with two rows of needles. Both sides may look the same. Double knit has body and limited stretch. It should be used for more tailored garments such as dresses, pants and suits.

Sweater knits can be made on a single or a double knit machine. They are usually made from a heavier yarn and are loosely knitted.

Some other knits that are widely used are rib knit, interlock and warp knits.

Rib knits have vertical ribs alternating on both sides of the fabric which provide a great amount of stretch in the crosswise direction. Ribbing should be used for neckbands, cuffs, waistbands. It can also be used for ribbing tops but be sure to use a pattern that is designed especially for ribbing. Ribbing usually stretches 100% crosswise.

Interlock is made on a circular knitting machine by inter-locking stitches. It is similar to jersey but both sides usually look the same. This fabric is suitable for blouses, dresses, evening pants and some styles of skirts.

Warp knit is constructed on a special machine which uses many yarns that form loops simultaneously in the lengthwise (warp) direction. The fabric has limited stretch. Warp knits can be obtained in light to medium weight.

All synthetic fabrics should be washed often and should not be permitted to get too soiled. Try to separate the colored garments from the white, as there is a tendency for the white to pick up the colors from the colored garments. Do not wash man-made fiber in hot water. If there is any doubt in your mind concerning the content of the fabric, that is, whether it is natural or man-made, you can utilize the flame test. Burn a small piece of thread. Natural fibers smell and burn with a flame leaving a very soft ash. Synthetic fibers melt and leave a hard ash.

It is important to know how to take care of a garment and the following should be helpful:

Polyester fibers are known by many names, some of which are Dacron, Trevira, Kodel, Terylene, Fortrel, Vycron, Encron. Usually this fabric can be hand or machine washed using a warm setting. They can be dried in a dryer, but you should be careful to remove them promptly as they will get wrinkled if they remain in the dryer for too long a period. Usually all garments made from this fiber can be dry cleaned.

Acrylic fibers are known under the names Orlon, Acrilan, Courtelle, Dralon, Creslan and Dynel. Most of the fabric made from these type of fibers can be washed by hand or by machine in cold or warm water. You should use a low temperature setting when drying them, and they should be removed immediately to avoid wrinkles and static electricity.

When washing garments made from either polyester or acrylic fabrics, we suggest that you turn the garment inside out to avoid snags in the polyester and pilling in the acrylic.

We suggest that all woolen garments be dry cleaned. However, some dry cleaners do a much better job than others when pressing. If in doubt have the garment dry cleaned only and do the pressing yourself.

As cotton has a tendency to shrink, make sure to wash the fabric before you cut out the garment unless the label indicates that the fabric has been preshrunk at the mill.

To be on the safe side, we recommend that you preshrink all fabric before you cut out the garment. When you pre-wash the fabric, use the same settings on the washer and dryer that you will use when you wash the finished garment. It is very discouraging to go to all the work of constructing a garment only to find that it has shrunk after the first washing.

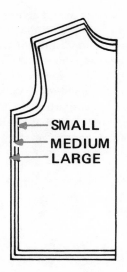

SMALL
MEDIUM
LARGE

PATTERNS

When working with knit and stretch fabric, it is very important to use patterns designed especially for these fabrics. If you use a pattern designed for non-stretch fabric, you will end up with a garment which is too large for you. All the patterns referred to in this book are made by KWIK·SEW Pattern Co. KWIK·SEW has patterns designed for both stretch and non-stretch fabric.

Before you buy the fabric, select the pattern as each pattern indicates what type of fabric is necessary and how much fabric is required. These patterns also indicate what notions are required, etc.

Three to four sizes are included in each envelope and each size is marked in a different color, making it very easy for you to cut out the correct size.

Complete, easy-to-follow instructions are included with each pattern as well as instructions on how to properly set your sewing machine so that it will sew these fabrics. Even if you are making your first garment or if you are an inexperienced sewer, you should have no difficulty in obtaining a very professional looking garment.

KWIK·SEW patterns are sized using the United States Government sizing specifications. To be certain that you are obtaining the correct size, check the sizes on the back of the pattern envelope and compare these with the actual body measurements. A certain amount of ease is included in the patterns. The amount of ease varies according to the design of the pattern, the style and type of garment and the type of fabric to be used. For example, a pattern for non-stretch fabric includes more ease than a pattern for stretch fabric. The pattern pieces for a swimsuit designed for stretch fabric are actually smaller than your body measurements. This is necessary so that the swimsuit will fit properly.

When you are using patterns designed for stretch fabric, it is important to use the fabric with the correct degree of stretch. To determine the correct amount of stretch, use the stretch chart. Fold the fabric double and gently stretch the fabric. Do not stretch the fabric so tight that the fabric rolls excessively. This is also a good time to check the fabric for recovery. If the fabric does not go back to its original shape after being stretched, it will probably mean that the fabric will sag and stretch out of shape when the garment is worn.

Fabric with 18% stretch across the grain such as: Single knit, Double knit

4" of Knit Fabric should stretch	to at least here. →

Fabric with 25% stretch across the grain such as: Nylon tricot, Nylon sheer, Interlock, Velour

4" of Knit Fabric should stretch	to at least here. →

Fabric with 35% stretch across the grain such as: Sweater fabric, Velour, Terry, Interlock, Fabric with Spandex or Lycra

4" of Knit Fabric should stretch	to at least here. →

Fabric with 50% stretch such as: Swimsuit fabric, Fabric with Spandex or Lycra

4" of Knit Fabric should stretch	to at least here. →

Fabric with 70% stretch such as: Swimsuit fabric, Power net (Girdle fabric)

4" of Knit Fabric should stretch	to at least here. →

Fabric with 100% stretch across the grain such as: Ribbing

4" of Knit Fabric should stretch	to at least here. →

KWIK·SEW has a complete assortment of sizes from babies to king and queen size.

Many patterns, especially for T-shirts and sweaters, are sized as small, medium, large and extra large. As these patterns are not form fitted and because of the stretch factor in the fabric, more than one size is covered in each classification. For example, size "Small" is equal to Size 8 and 10. "Medium" is equal to Size 12 and 14, "Large" equals Size 16 and 18, "Extra Large" equals 20 to 22.

KWIK·SEW patterns are carried by most leading fabric stores in the United States, Canada and Australia. If your store does not have the patterns, they can obtain them for you.

BODY MEASUREMENTS

When you are selecting a pattern, be sure to take your body measurements and compare them with the ones on the back of the pattern envelope.

After you have taken your measurements, buy a pattern as close as possible to these measurements as too many changes will cause you a lot of additional work.

The first step before you change a pattern is to know your own measurements. You cannot do this yourself; have a friend measure you. Wear the proper undergarments and correct shoes when you are being measured.

Use the following guide to take the body measurements:

BUST

The bust measurement is taken by placing the tape measure over the back, underneath the arm and then over the highest point on the bust. The tape measure should be higher in the back than in the front. Note illustration. Do not pull the tape measure too tightly; this should be an exact measurement, not too tight and not too loose.

WAIST

The next measurement is the waist. Tie a string around your waist to determine the location of your waist. Here it is very important not to follow the natural tendency to have a small waist and thus pull the tape measure too tightly. The waist measurement varies and this should also be taken into consideration. You should be able to slip a couple of fingers between the tape and your waist when you take the measurement.

HIP

The hip measurement is taken over the widest portion of the hips. Measure the distance from your waist to the widest part of your hips. This distance varies considerably but it is usually between 8″ (20 cm) and 10″ (25 cm). This measurement is very important when you are constructing a pair of fitted slacks or a skirt.

13

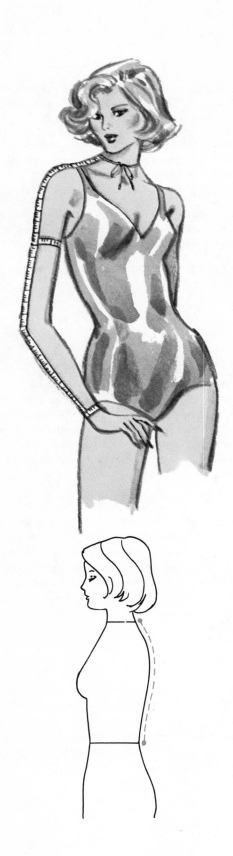

SHOULDER AND ARM LENGTH

To determine the shoulder measurement and arm length, tie a string around your neck to determine the neckline. Measure the shoulder width from the string to the bone at the tip of the shoulder. Write down this measurement.

With the tape measure in this position, measure over your elbow down to your wrist bone. Bend your arm slightly so the tape measure goes over the elbow.

Deduct the shoulder width from the total amount and you will obtain your arm length. The arms of many people are not the same length so measure both arms and take any difference into consideration when adjusting your sleeve length.

UPPER ARM AND WRIST

Measure the circumference of your arm around the widest part of the upper arm. Also measure around your wrist bone. These measurements are necessary if you are constructing a garment with a fitted sleeve.

BACK LENGTH

The length of your back should be measured from the top of your backbone down to your natural waistline.

BACK WIDTH

The back width is measured across the back between the arms. Do not measure underneath the arms.

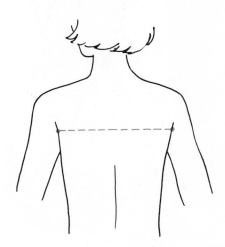

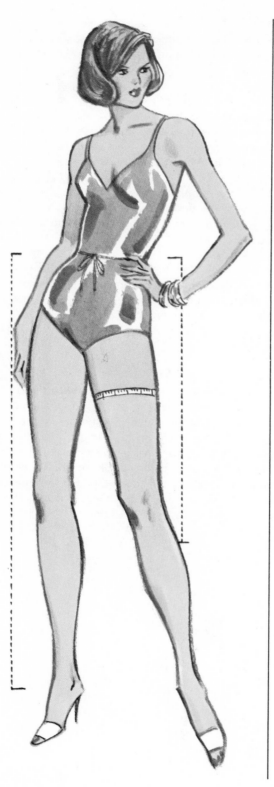

LENGTH

The length of the skirt is measured from the waist down to the length you wish the skirt to be.

For the length of your slacks, measure at your side, from the waist over your hip bone to the length you wish the slacks to be.

To obtain your crotch measurement, sit up straight on a flat table or on a hard chair which does not have any curves in the seat. Measure from the waist over the hip to the top of the table or chair.

If you are constructing a pair of slacks, you have to know the measurement of your legs at the fullest part of your thighs.

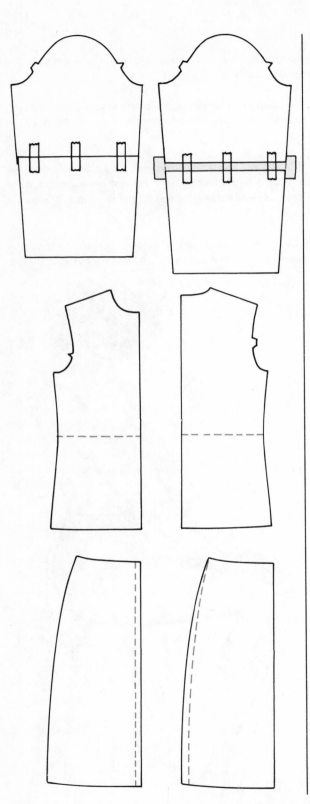

LENGTHEN OR SHORTEN

If you have to lengthen or shorten a pattern you never lengthen or shorten it at the bottom as this will alter the design line.

To change the length of a sleeve, cut across the pattern piece slightly lower than the elbow. Adjust the length by either overlapping the pattern to shorten the sleeve or tape a strip of paper to lengthen the sleeve. Do not forget to allow for the hem and the seam allowance.

To change the length on a top, cut the pattern piece apart halfway between the underarm and the waist. Make sure that you made the same adjustment on both the front and back pattern pieces.

To shorten or lengthen the skirt length you follow the above procedure. Cut across the pattern piece slightly lower than the widest part of your hips or follow the shorten and lengthen lines on the pattern.

WIDTH ADJUSTMENT

If you have to widen a skirt or make the skirt smaller, the easiest way is to increase or decrease at the center front and center back. When you check the size of the pattern, always remember to measure inside the pattern seam allowance. You can also change the width of the pattern at the side seams both in the back and in the front. The adjustment has to be a curved line following the curve in the pattern.

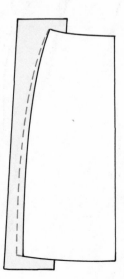

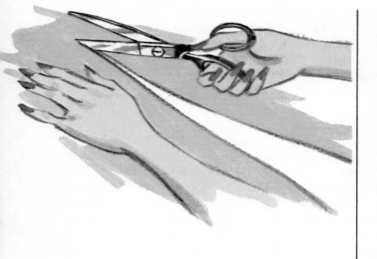

CUTTING

As many stretch fabrics are made from synthetic fibers, you will find that your scissors will become dull quicker than when cutting natural fibers. It is very important to have a clean cut. So make sure you start out with a pair of sharp scissors and if they should become dull, get them sharpened as soon as possible. As some stretch fabric is very stretchy, dull scissors have a tendency to "chew" the fabric rather than cut it. This is especially true with sweater fabric. The special technique for cutting sweater fabric may be found in Section III. When the pattern calls for a ¼" (6 mm) seam allowance, it is very important that you have a clean cut.

Before cutting the garment, check to make sure that the length is correct. This is the most common adjustment on any pattern. If any major adjustment has to be made on the pattern and you are not sure how to make the adjustment, refer to the book, PROFESSIONAL PATTERN ALTERATIONS MADE EASY, published by KWIK·SEW Pattern Co., Inc.

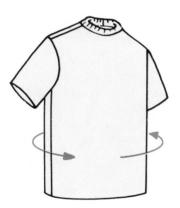

When cutting out a garment using stretch fabric, you have to be sure that the stretch goes around the body. If you do not do this you will end up with a garment that is long and narrow after it has been used a few times. This is especially true when you use loosely knitted fabric. If you are using two-way stretch fabric, the fabric will always stretch more in one direction than the other. The greatest amount of stretch goes around the body.

Before cutting out the fabric the usual procedure is to place the fabric double right side to right side. However, sometimes it is necessary to cut some of the pattern pieces out of a single thickness of fabric. In this way you can often save on the amount of fabric you use. So, before you cut out any of the pieces, place all the pattern pieces on the fabric and figure out how to proceed.

Most patterns have a layout for cutting included in the instructions. Follow the layout given for your size, view and fabric width. Any changes you make on the pattern, such as lengthening, etc., can change the position of the pattern pieces. In this case, use the layout only as a guide.

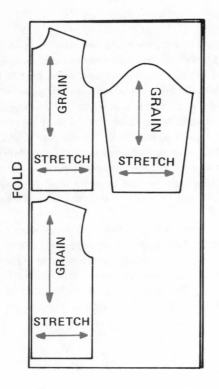

Make sure the fold is along the grain in order to insure a proper fit. As you are working with fabric that stretches, try to keep the fabric on top of the table and not hanging down as this will tend to pull it out of shape and the pieces will not be identical with the pattern.

Regardless of the garment you are making, always be sure to follow the arrows on the pattern pieces to make sure you have the grain and stretch of the fabric in the right directions. When you pin the pattern to the fabric, there is a possibility, when working with fine knits, that you will have runs if a dull pin cuts the thread in a loop. Because of this, it is very important that you use very fine pins with sharp points when you pin the pattern to the fabric. Some people prefer to use weights to hold the pattern pieces in place. Ashtrays, cups, etc., will do very nicely as long as they keep the pattern steady on the fabric.

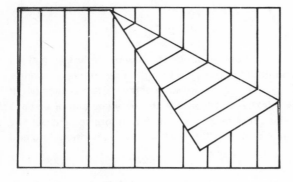

If you are using striped or plaid fabric, it is very important to line up the stripes before you start cutting. Also, if you wish to change the seam allowances, this should be taken into consideration before you start cutting.

Before you cut out the fabric, you should be sure to press out the creases. Make sure that your iron is set for the correct temperature. Sometimes you will find polyester fabric that has a crease which you cannot remove. In this case, make sure when you cut out the pattern, that this crease ends up in an inconspicuous place.

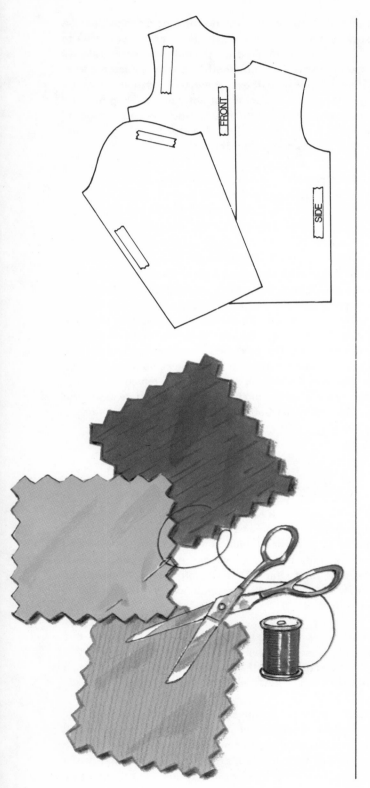

When you have cut out the pattern pieces, it is a good idea to mark each piece so that you do not mix them up. We recommend using transparent tape. This is the type of tape which you can sew through without the backing on the tape sticking to the needle. Place a small piece on the wrong side of the fabric marking the side seams, back, etc. This tape has a dull finish which you can write on. Always use a pencil, as a ballpoint pen could spot the garment and these spots are very difficult to wash out.

This tape can also be used for basting and has many other useful applications. As you read on you will find how this is done, plus you will discover many other shortcuts that rely on this tape. Be careful when you are using transparent tape on velour, stretch terry cloth or other fabric with a similar surface, as it may mark the fabric. Try the tape on a piece of scrap fabric before you use it.

THREAD

The proper thread is very important when sewing. As knit fabric stretches, you should use a thread that also stretches with the fabric and returns to normal when the "stretch" is relaxed. There are many threads that do this. However, some have very obvious disadvantages. An example of this is nylon monofilament thread. (This is very similar to the monofilament fishing line used with spin tackle.) The trouble with this thread is that it is very stiff and greatly increases the possibility of skipped stitches. The reason some sewers use this thread is because it has no color of its own and can be used with any color of fabric as it tends to take on the color of the fabric. Another disadvantage of this thread is that it is very hard on the sewing machine as it cuts grooves in the tension discs.

There are many excellent threads on the market that have been developed especially for stretch sewing. These threads are color fast and extremely strong. This strength is very important, for example, in making the crotch seam in a pair of slacks. The advantage of these threads is that they have "controlled stretch". This is essential when sewing stretch fabric. In addition, they are very fine threads which are necessary for sewing lightweight fabric. Yet, because of their great strength, you can also use them for sewing heavy fabrics. These threads can also be used in all types of sewing as they are fade-resistant and will not shrink. They come in a variety of colors. Regardless of the type of thread you are using, always be sure to use the same thread on the top of the sewing machine as you use on the bobbin.

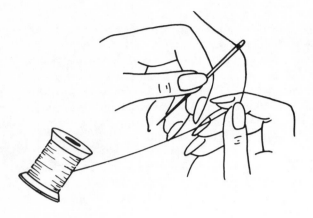

Almost all functions, when using knit fabric, can be done on a sewing machine. However, in some cases, you have to sew a few stitches by hand and the following should always be kept in mind. All synthetic thread is manufactured from synthetic fibers and these fibers tend to revert to their original shape. It is very important when sewing by hand that you always thread the needle from the end coming off the spool. If you do not follow this procedure, you will end up with small knots in the thread.

NORMAL TENSION

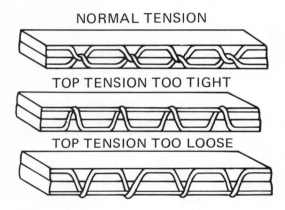

TOP TENSION TOO TIGHT

TOP TENSION TOO LOOSE

SEWING

Before you start sewing, take a small piece of scrap fabric, double the fabric, and sew a straight stitch. Check the stitches to be sure the tensions are correct. The perfect thread tension results when the top and bottom tensions are exactly equal and the knot is buried in the fabric and cannot be seen. The best rule to follow is to adjust the tensions so that the stitch appears the same on both sides. See diagram. Try to adjust only the top tension as this is easier to do on all sewing machines, but in some cases you may have to adjust both the top and bottom tensions.

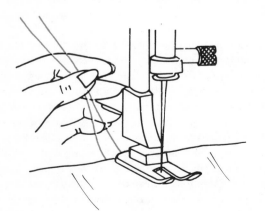

You will find it much easier to start a seam if you lower the needle into the fabric and hold both the top and bottom threads in your hand behind the presser foot. As the machine starts to sew, slowly pull these threads towards the rear of the machine. This will help the machine feed the material and eliminate the tendency of the material to bunch up under the presser foot.

If your sewing machine has a tendency to skip stitches, this is usually caused by a dull or bent needle. The first thing you should do is to change the needle. We recommend using a fine needle No. 10(70) or 12(80) for knit fabric.

If your machine continues to skip stitches and you are sewing on knit fabrics, we recommend that you use a ball point needle. This type of needle has a slightly rounded point and, as a result, it tends to go between the fabric yarns rather than piercing the yarn and causing it to split or break.

It is also very important to use the correct pressure on the presser foot. Most of the up-to-date machines can be adjusted which is usually simple to do. For woven and non-stretch fabric, you should use normal pressure on the presser foot. For loosely knitted and very stretchy fabric, you should loosen the pressure slightly on the presser foot.

It is sometimes difficult to sew sweater fabric with a regular presser foot. The loops in the fabric get caught on the presser foot and the fabric bunches up under the presser foot. A roller presser foot will eliminate this problem. The foot rolls over the fabric and you never have to worry that the fabric will bunch up under the roller presser foot.

When sewing single knit, either cotton or synthetic in lightweight material, we do not recommend a roller presser foot as the seam will have a tendency to pucker. The reason for this is that the rollers keep the bottom of the foot from touching the needle plate. Therefore, when you sew on thin fabric there is no pressure on the fabric where the needle enters it.

SEAMS

You can construct a garment in knit fabric on any kind of sewing machine using any type of stitch but naturally, some stitches are more suitable than others as the seam must be strong enough to hold when the fabric is stretched. The best stitches for making this kind of garment are found on the more sophisticated sewing machines which have reverse cycles. These machines produce stitches which stretch with the fabric. The type of stitch used depends upon the width of the seam allowance.

When using a reverse cycle machine, the best stitch to use when the seam allowance is ¼" (6 mm) is the overlock stitch, which sews the seam and overcasts in one operation. This is a stretch stitch so you do not have to stretch the fabric while sewing. This stitch saves you a great amount of time as you do not have to sew the seam twice.

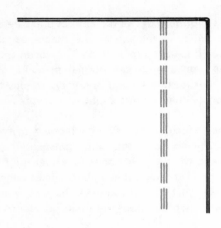

When using a ½" (1.3 cm) or ⅝" (1.5 cm) seam allowance, we recommend that you use a straight stitch. If you have a reverse cycle sewing machine, we recommend using an elastic straight stitch in stress areas such as the crotch and the seam used to sew in the sleeve. The machine sews two stitches forward and one stitch in reverse. This is a triple lock stitch which makes the seam stronger and more elastic.

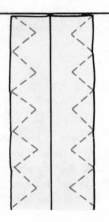

If the fabric requires overcasting, you should overcast the edges separately by using a three-step zigzag stitch. This is a stitch where the machine sews three stitches in each zig and each zag or use a large zigzag stitch.

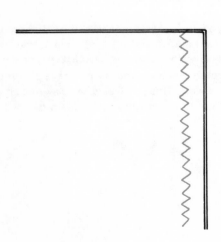

If you are using a regular zigzag machine, you should sew the seams with a narrow zigzag stitch when using a ¼" (6 mm) seam allowance. Set the stitch length at medium and the width at slightly less than medium.

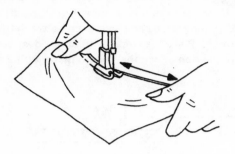

If you are using a straight stitch machine, you will have to follow different rules which will depend upon what type of fabric you are sewing. If you are working with sweater and single knit fabric, you should stretch the fabric in front and in back of the needle as you sew. Use a medium stitch length and sew two or three seams close together. Overcast the edges by hand. If you are working with double knit, it is usually not necessary to stretch the fabric. This will depend upon the fabric. However, you should stretch the fabric and sew two seams close together when you are sewing the crotch seam or sewing in a sleeve. This is also recommended for other places such as the elbow of a sleeve where there will be a greater degree of strain.

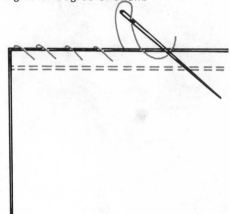

HEMMING

The fastest and easiest way to hem a garment made from knit fabric is to use an elastic blind stitch. This stitch will stretch with the fabric and will be invisible on the right side.

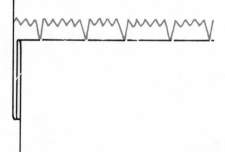

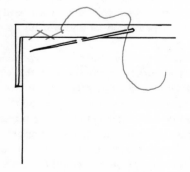

If your sewing machine does not have this kind of stitch, sew up the hem by hand. Be careful not to stitch on the very edge of the fabric. Stitch under the edge about ¼" (6 mm). Do not pull the thread very tightly as you sew as this will pucker the fabric.

On some fabrics fusible webbing can be used for hemming. Before using the fusible webbing, try it on a scrap piece of fabric that is the same as the garment. Cut strips of fusible webbing ¼" (6 mm) wide and place them between the hem and the garment. Place the strips ¼" (6 mm) down from the raw edge of the hem. Fuse the hem in place with a steam iron.

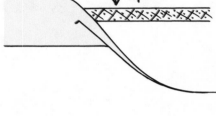

PRESSING

When sewing knit and stretch fabric, it is very important to press each seam as it is sewn. You have to press the garment in the correct way so that you will end up with a garment that looks professional and not home made.

It is also very important to use the correct type of iron and to set it at the temperature recommended for the fabric which you are using. If you are not sure of the content of the fabric, always use a cooler setting so that you are on the safe side. A hot iron used on polyester will melt the fabric; used on wool it could burn the material. This is so important that the American Wool Council suggests that you set your iron for "rayon" as the setting for "wool" is too hot on most irons.

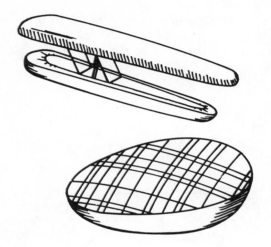

A steam iron gives much better results when working with knit and stretch fabrics. This is especially true when pressing sweater fabric. The steam does the work in shaping the garment.

The difference between ironing and pressing is that ironing is running the iron over the fabric in long back and forth strokes using pressure to remove creases and wrinkles in the fabric. Pressing is a press-lift, press-lift motion. You are applying both steam and heat to gently form the garment. When working with sweater fabric, the iron should actually not touch the fabric. The heat and steam do the work.

A pressing ham is very helpful, especially for form pressing the neckline on sweaters and T-shirts. It is also useful when form pressing a dart, shoulder cap, and all other areas which have to be formed. A sleeve board is also very useful for pressing the sleeve seams. Most pressing is done from the wrong side of the garment. Quite often, to obtain a finished look, you have to press from the right side. When doing this, we recommend that you use a pressing cloth; otherwise you may end up with shiny seams.

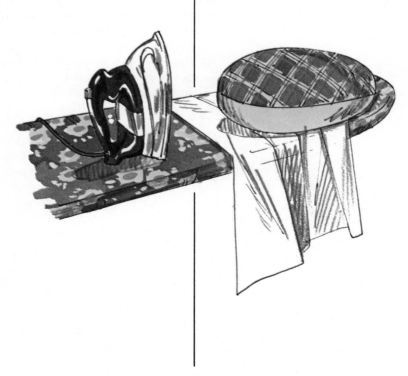

Before you cut out the fabric, you should be sure to press out the creases. Again, make sure that your iron is set for the correct temperature.

When you are pressing a seam using ¼'' (6 mm) seam allowance, first press the seam flat in the same grain direction as it was sewn. Now, press the seam allowance toward one side.

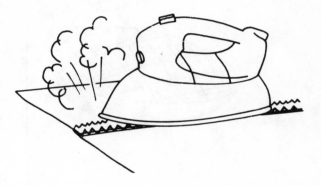

Even when using a larger seam allowance, always press the seam flat and then open the seam allowance and press it open. Sometimes when you press open a seam the seam allowance will leave an imprint which shows on the right side. To eliminate this imprint, place a strip of paper under the seam allowance before you press it. Or, after you have pressed the seam, gently press under the edge of the seam allowance.

When pressing a hem you have to make sure that you do not press over the stitches as this will leave a line on the right side. Press the hem but do not press over the stitches. Then, on the wrong side, press under the hem edge. This will give you a hem which is invisible from the right side. Another method is to press the hem before you sew it.

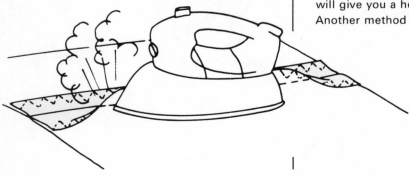

knit tops and t-shirts

A knit top or a T-shirt is a type of garment that can be worn by the entire family whether you live in a hot climate, where it is worn outside, or in a cold area where it can be used as an informal indoor shirt.

In addition to their many uses, these garments have the added advantage of being one of the easiest items to construct. At one time you could only use cotton knit for the shirt; now, however, you can find fiber combinations which have many advantages over 100 percent cotton, i.e., 50 percent polyester and 50 percent cotton or 40 percent polyester and 60 percent cotton or many other combinations. All of these or other combinations will not shrink to the same degree as cotton.

If you are not certain of the content, or, if you do not know the shrinkage factor, always be on the safe side by preshrinking in hot water before proceeding.

Single knit is the most suitable for this type of garment as it is usually a lighter weight than double knit. Single or double needle is the method used to knit the fabric. The easiest way to tell the difference is to look on both sides of the fabric. Single knit looks smooth and finished on the right side only, while double knit looks almost the same on both sides in addition to being heavier.

Some people believe that single knit fabrics are always smooth and do not have any texture. This is no longer true. Machines have now been developed which give us beautiful finishes in a wide variety of textures.

Single knit usually comes in a double width, approximately 60'' (152 cm) wide. Because this fabric tends to roll at the edges, it is doubled and the edges knitted or sewn together at the mill. This makes it easier for the manufacturer or fabric stores to handle the rolls or bolts. Some single knit is knitted in a tubular shape. It is often difficult to see where the edges are joined. In some instances, it looks like a flaw. This is where you should cut the material apart before proceeding. This will eliminate the possibility of ending up with this seam or flaw in the front or back, etc., where it will be very noticeable.

You should also be careful, when cutting out the garment, that the crease in the fabric is not in a conspicuous place as this crease is very often difficult to press out.

KWIK·SEW patterns for T-shirts are available with either raglan sleeves or set-in sleeves. They also have patterns for knit tops. The difference between a knit top and T-shirt pattern is the design as some knit tops have darts and are more fitted. In addition, the pattern has various styles and sleeve variations. The T-shirt does not have any darts and it is a garment which hangs loosely. This is one of the reasons it is so popular. The most common style is with a simple round neck. The sleeves can be either short or long.

Regardless of the type of sleeve you choose to use, a T-shirt is one of the easiest garments to construct. Also, this is an ideal item for a child to try to sew. The material is inexpensive, it can be sewn quickly, and she will have the thrill of sewing her own clothes with a minimum of supervision on your part. Perhaps this will be the start of her interest in sewing, an interest that in the years to come will give her tremendous satisfaction and will give you tremendous savings.

Always check your measurements with the pattern so that you will get the correct length for both the body and the sleeves. Fold the fabric double, with the right sides together. Place the pattern pieces on the fabric and be sure to always follow the arrows on the pattern pieces as it is very important that the greatest degree of stretch goes around the body and around the arms.

To make this garment, use a ¼'' (6 mm) seam allowance as this is included in the pattern.

Whenever possible, use ribbing for the neck opening and the cuffs. This gives a more professional look to the garment. It is often more desirable not to use the same color as the body. This is what gives you variation, a contrasting color often looks sharp, or you can use the same color as a skirt or a pair of slacks to create a matching ensemble. Here is an opportunity for you to use your imagination and really be creative. Why don't you try ribbing with small checks or stripes?

When cutting out the pattern pieces, be sure to use a sharp pair of scissors and use a fine needle as a heavy needle sometimes cuts the yarn which causes small "runs" at the seams. This very simple garment can be sewn together using almost any kind of stitch. If you are using a plain straight stitch, set the stitch length at medium. Remember to stretch the fabric as you sew. This will give you a more elastic seam. It is a good idea to sew a second seam close to the raw edges to keep the fabric from rolling. A zigzag stitch is better than a straight stitch. Set the width for slightly less than medium and the length of the stitch for medium.

Some of these fabrics have a tendency to run. Other types do not and as this is a garment you wash very often, we recommend that you overcast the edges. Either use a large zigzag stitch or use a three-step zigzag stitch.

The most timesaving stitch to use is an overlock stitch which allows you to sew the garment together and overcast in one operation. Up until a short time ago, this type of seam was only possible on commercial sewing machines. However, there have been great improvements in home sewing machines and some of the most up-to-date machines made for home use can now perform these more complicated stitches.

T-SHIRT WITH SET-IN SLEEVES

Start constructing a T-shirt with set-in sleeves by placing the back and the front, right side to right side, and sew the shoulder seams.

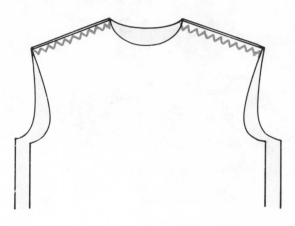

Finish the neck opening before you proceed with the rest of the garment. For the neck opening, cut a straight piece of ribbing across the grain 2½" (6.5 cm) wide or as wide as desired. As the stretch factor in the ribbing varies considerably, you are always on the safe side if you cut a length 18" (46 cm) long.

A pattern piece for the neckband is included in the pattern. Some patterns give the exact size of the neckband, others give the maximum length you will need.

To get the correct size for the neckband, stretch the band tightly around the head. Be sure that you can pull the neckband over the head. As some fabric is very stretchy, make sure that the band is not so short that it will choke when placed around the neck. Cut off the excess fabric.

If you are constructing a garment for someone else and you cannot obtain the head measurement, measure your own head as the heads of all people are very much similar in size.

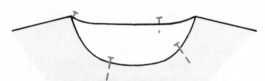

Dividing neckline with
seam at shoulders

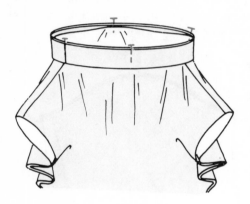

Sew the ends of this band together to form a circle by folding right side to right side. Fold and press band lengthwise, wrong sides together. Divide neckband and neck opening in fourths with pins.

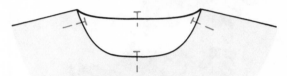

Dividing neckline with
seam at center back

Pin band to neck opening on right side, raw edges together, matching pins.

Place the seams on the neckband at one shoulder seam; or if you are making a child's T-shirt, place the seam at the center of the back. When sewing the neckband onto the shirt, stretch the neckband between the pins so that it will fit the neck opening. The easiest way to do this is to always have the smallest piece on top. In this case the neck opening is underneath and the neckband on top. When using stretch fabric you always stretch the smaller piece to fit the larger. This is the opposite method used for sewing non-stretch fabric where you always ease the larger piece to fit the smaller.

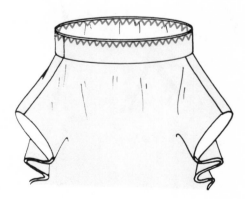

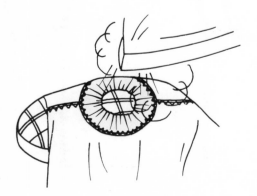

To obtain a professional looking neckline, it is very important to press the neckline after you have sewn on the neckband. Place the neckline over a pressing ham and steam press the neckline into shape.

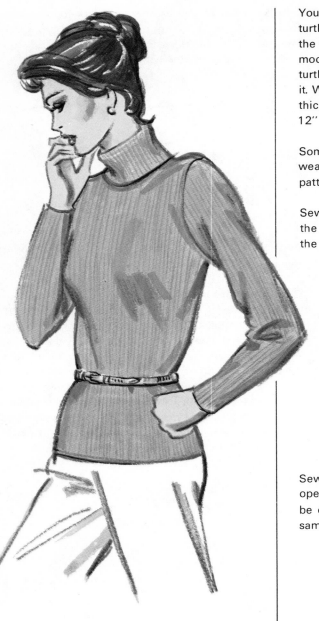

You use the same procedure for a turtleneck or a mock turtleneck as used for the round neck; the only difference is the width of the neckband. The most common width for a mock turtle neckband is 4½'' (11 cm). The width of a turtleneck depends upon how many times you wish to fold it. We suggest that you make the neckband using a double thickness of fabric and the width should be 10'' (26 cm) to 12'' (31 cm).

Some of the shortcuts used by manufacturers of ready-to-wear garments have been incorporated into KWIK·SEW patterns and the following is one of these shortcuts:

Sew the sleeves in place before you sew the side seams and the sleeve seams. Match the top center of the sleeve with the shoulder seam and the underarm edges.

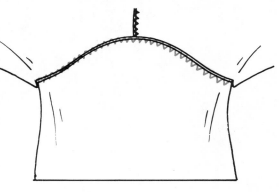

Sew side seam and sleeve seam in one continuous operation, starting at the bottom of the shirt. The sleeves can be either long or short; they both can be finished in the same way.

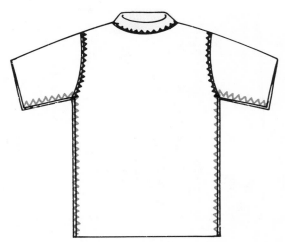

Hem the sleeves and the bottom of the shirt at the desired hemline by folding the hem to the wrong side. You can hem the shirt either by hand or by machine. You can use either a blind stitch or a regular seam. Or, you may wish to finish the sleeve by attaching a cuff. Use ribbing cut across the grain twice as wide as you want the finished cuff to be plus seam allowances. Remember that the width of the finished cuff will add that amount to the length of the sleeve. Or you can purchase ready-made cuffs. You can also use self-fabric. Cut across the grain if it has enough stretch. Regardless of what you use, the construction is the same.

Measure around the arm where the cuff will be. To get the correct size, stretch the ribbing around the arm so that it feels comfortable. Cut off the excess ribbing. Sew ends of the cuffs together to form circles. Fold and press each band lengthwise, wrong sides together. Divide cuffs and sleeve openings in fourths with pins.

Pin cuffs to sleeve openings, right sides and raw edges together, matching pins. Sew the cuffs on, stretching the cuffs to fit the sleeve opening.

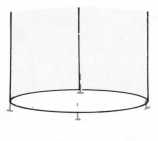

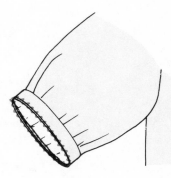

T-SHIRT WITH RAGLAN SLEEVES

It is just as easy to construct a T-shirt with raglan sleeves as it is when using a set-in sleeve. There is only one thing you should watch out for. The back and front raglan seams are different lengths. An easy way to eliminate any errors is to mark each piece with transparent tape and label each piece with a pencil.

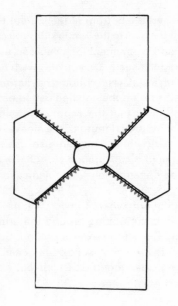

After sewing the back and front shoulder seams, the T-shirt should look like the diagram.

Sew on the neckband using the same procedure as used for the set-in sleeve.

Sew the side seam and the sleeve seam in one continuous operation.

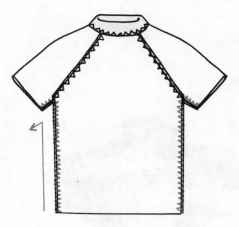

Use the same procedure for finishing the sleeves and bottom as described for the set-in sleeve T-shirt.

A variety of patterns can be found for knit tops. The construction is basically the same as for a T-shirt except for certain instances which call for a bust dart. Start the construction by sewing the darts in place. Start from the widest part of the dart as it is easier to get a smooth finish at the point of the dart.

It is sometimes difficult to sew a straight line for a dart when it is sewn on the bias. Place a piece of tape along the edge of the dart line and use the edge of the tape as a guide line when sewing the dart.

If you are constructing a knit top with a scoop neck or a crew neck, follow the same procedure as for a round neck on a T-shirt. Be sure to use the correct length for the neckband.

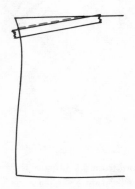

SELF-FABRIC NECKBAND

It is not necessary to use ribbing for the neckband , self-fabric may be used. The neckband has to be cut across the grain. It is also necessary to slightly lower the neckline so that you can pull the T-shirt over your head. On the pattern piece, make a mark at the center front ½" (1.3 cm) down from the neck opening. Make another mark ¼" (6 mm) in from the neckline at the shoulder. At the center back, make a mark ¼" (6 mm) down from the neckline. On both the front and the back pattern pieces, draw a smooth curved line from the shoulder to the center front and from the shoulder to the center back.

To determine the length of the neckband, measure the neck opening, cut the neckband 1½" (3.8 cm) smaller than the neck opening. Be sure that the neckband is large enough to go over your head. Attach the neckband in the same way as previously described.

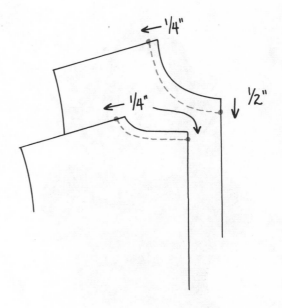

NECK VARIATIONS

When sewing on the neckband for a T-shirt, you can use a different method than previously described. After you have divided the neckband and the neck opening in fourths with pins, pin the right side of the neckband to the wrong side of the neck opening, placing the raw edges together, matching the pins. Sew on the band.

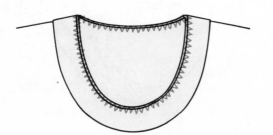

Fold the neckline seam allowance towards the shirt. Topstitch through the shirt and the seam allowance close to the seam. This prevents the shirt from rolling to the outside. Fold the neckband on the seam line to the outside of the shirt. Topstitch the neckband to the shirt close to the folded edge of the neckband. If desired, topstitch again ¼'' (6 mm) up from the first seam.

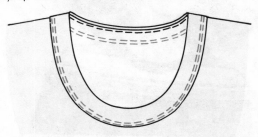

Press the neckline so that it lies flat. This same method can be used to finish the sleeve openings.

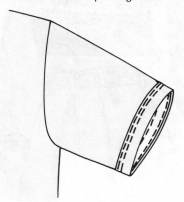

Instead of using a straight stitch for topstitching, you may also use a decorative stitch. As a variation, especially for a little girl's T-shirt, place a strip of lace underneath the neckband so that the lace is protruding and topstitch the lace in place.

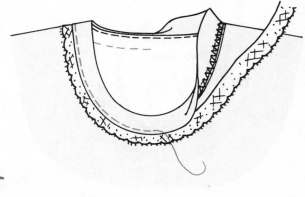

ROUND NECK WITH SLIT FRONT

For a simple variation for a T-shirt, you can make a round neck with a slit front. When you are cutting out the fabric, cut a slit at the center front 5½'' (14 cm) down from the neck opening. Cut two slit bands ½'' (1.3 cm) longer than the slit. The stretch of the fabric should be lengthwise. The bands should be 1¼'' (3.2 cm) wide. For the neckband and the tie, cut a strip of fabric 48'' (122 cm) long and 1¼'' (3.2 cm) wide. Again, the stretch of the fabric should be lengthwise. Staystitch the bottom edge of the slit ¼'' (6 mm) on each side and across the bottom edge.

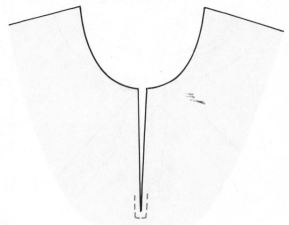

Pin the right side of the slit band to the wrong side of each side of the slit opening. Sew from the neckline to the end of the staystitching ¼'' (6 mm) down from the slit opening. On the front, clip the shirt to the corners to make it easier to turn.

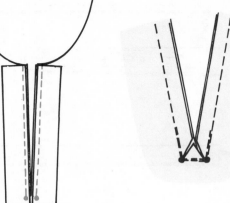

Fold the slit band over the seam allowance to the right side, fold the edges under ¼'' (6 mm) and pin to cover the stitches. Topstitch close to the folded edge of the slit through all layers. Stop ¼'' (6 mm) from the end of the slit.

37

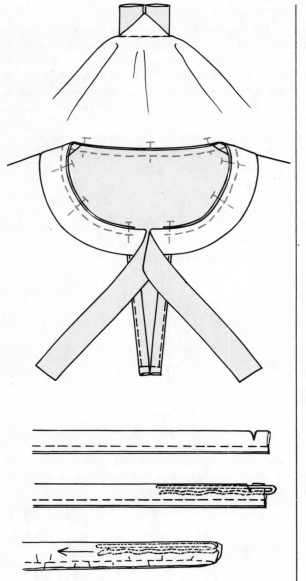

Tuck the ends of the bottom edge of the slit to the inside. From the inside, sew across the bands and the clipped triangle on the front. Sew the front to the back at the shoulder seams.

Divide the neckband in half, pin the right side of the neckband to the wrong side of the neck opening. Match the middle of the neckband to the center back with the front ties extending on both sides of the center front. Sew the neckband to the neck opening. Fold each tie double lengthwise with the right sides together. Sew the length of the ties stopping at the center front.

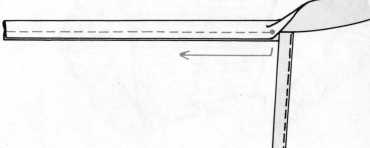

There are various ways for turning a tie right side out. The easiest way is to cut a little hole in the fold ½'' (1.3 cm) from the edge. Insert a bobby pin with smooth tips into the opening (hooked through the cut opening), guide the bobby pin to other end.

Another method of turning this narrow strip is to place a piece of string inside the strip before you sew it. Sew one end of the string to the fabric. Sew the seam with the string inside. Now pull on the string and you will turn the tie right side out.

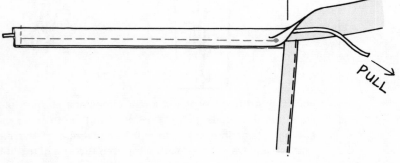

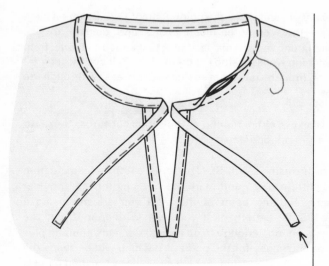

Around the neck opening, fold the neckband over the seam allowance to the right side. Fold under the raw edges and pin the neckband in place. Be sure to cover the stitches. Trim the tip of the ties and fold the raw edges to the inside. Topstitch all around the tie and the neck opening. Start at one end of the tie and continue to the other end.

V-NECK

If you plan to make a V-neck, proceed as follows: Always sew the shoulder seams before you construct the neck opening. The point of the V can be sewn in various ways. The vertical V and the overlap V are two of the most popular methods. The same procedure is used for both types of V-necks up to the point where you finish the point of the V.

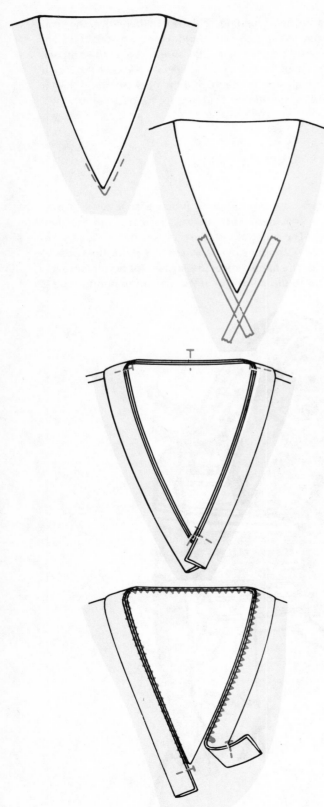

You should staystitch the point of the V 1" (2.5 cm) on each side. However, it is much easier and quicker to use transparent tape. This is done to keep the fabric from stretching while making the point of the V. Place the tape ⅜" (1 cm) from the raw edge so that you do not sew through the tape.

You can use either ribbing or self-fabric cut across the grain for a V-neck opening.

If you are using KWIK·SEW patterns, cut the neckband from the pattern piece and mark the notches for the shoulder seams and the point of the V. If you are not using a KWIK·SEW pattern or if you wish a deeper V, cut the neckband long enough to go around the neck opening plus seam allowance for the point of V which will be twice the width of the neckband. For example, if the finished band is 1" (2.5 cm) wide, cut the neckband 2" (5 cm) longer than the neck opening and 2½" (6.5 cm) wide.

Fold and press the neckband double lengthwise, wrong sides together. Pin the neckband to the neck opening on the right side with the raw edges together. Start pinning at the point of the V. Leave the neckband extending one inch. Pin the neckband around the neck opening.

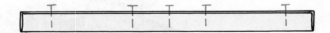

The neckband should be approximately ½" (1.3 cm) shorter than the neck opening from the point of the V to the shoulder and 1½" (3.8 cm) across the back neck opening.

OVERLAPPED V-NECK

For an overlap V, start sewing at the point of the V and sew all the way around, stopping at a distance from the point equal to the width of the neckband on the left front.

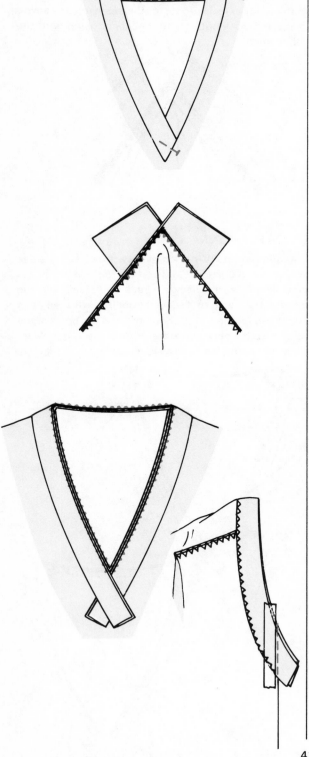

The proper overlap for a V-neck for a lady should come from the right side. This is the opposite from the way a man's V-neck is constructed.

Place the end of the band, which is sewn down to the point of the V, over the band on the other side. Insert the end of this band into the opening.

Secure both ends on the wrong side by sewing around the peak of the V. Cut off the ends of the band close to the stitches.

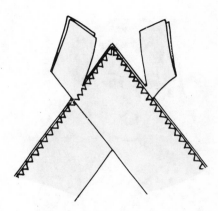

VERTICAL V-NECK

Sew on the neckband starting ⅛″ (3 mm) from the point of the V and sew all the way around stopping ⅛″ (3 mm) from the point of the V.

To obtain a correct V, fold the front right side to right side, making sure that the point of the V is lined up with the center fold.

Check to make sure that the neckbands are edge to edge. The ends of the neckband will extend approximately 1″ (2.5 cm) from the center fold. Place a piece of tape on the edge of the center fold and over the ends of the neckbands. Sew a seam on the neckband at the edge of the tape.

Remove the tape and press the seam open. Attach the ends of the neckband and finish the point by sewing a seam around the point of the V on top of the seam already sewn. Cut off the excess length of the neckband even with the seam allowance.

V-NECK WITH PIPING

Another variation for a V-neck may be achieved by the use of piping between the neckband and the top. Cut the piping the same length as the neckline plus 2″ (5 cm). Pin the piping to the right side of the neck opening, with the ends of the piping extending 1″ (2.5 cm) beyond the point of the V. Sew on the piping starting at the point of the V. It is easier to sew on the piping if you use a zipper foot.

POINT OF "V"

POINT OF "V"

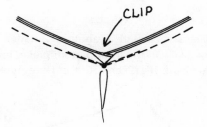

CLIP

Clip front to the point of the V. Press the seam allowance towards the shirt.

Fold the piping, right sides together, and sew across the piping along the center front. Open the seam on the piping as illustrated.

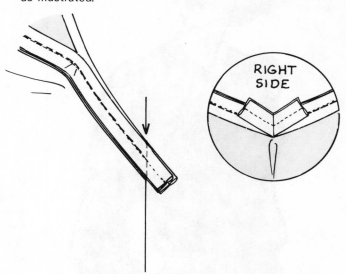

RIGHT SIDE

Fold the neckband, right side to right side, and sew the ends together. You have to be sure that the neckband is the correct size. Fold the neckband double, lengthwise and press. The seam on the neckband should be placed at the center back. Place a pin at the center front of the neckband. Pin the neckband to the right side of the neckline over the piping, matching the seam on the neckband to the center back and pin to the center front. Sew on the neckband on the same line of stitches as used for sewing on the piping. Use a zipper foot for this operation. Fold the front and the band, right sides together, along the center front. Sew the center front seam of the neckband from the outside edge of the band to the seam in line with the center front fold as illustrated. On the inside, open the seam and attach with a few stitches by hand.

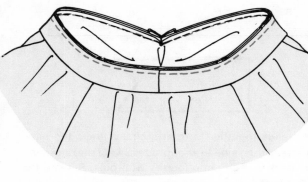

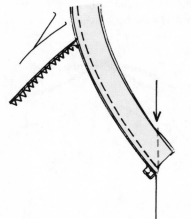

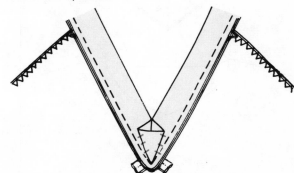

HEART SHAPED NECKBAND

The heart shaped neckband is another variation that is extremely attractive. On the front pattern piece, lower the center front neckline ¾″ (2 cm). Cut out the neckline as illustrated.

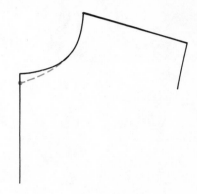

Cut a straight piece of ribbing across the grain 3″ (8 cm) wide. Use the same procedure for the correct neck measurement as you used for a regular round neck plus 1″ (2.5 cm). Cut each end of the band as illustrated.

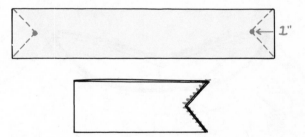

Sew the ends together to form a circle. Press the band lengthwise, wrong side to wrong side. Divide the neckband and the neck opening into fourths with pins. Sew on the neckband, matching the pins and the raw edges. The seam in the neckband should be placed at the center front.

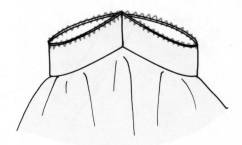

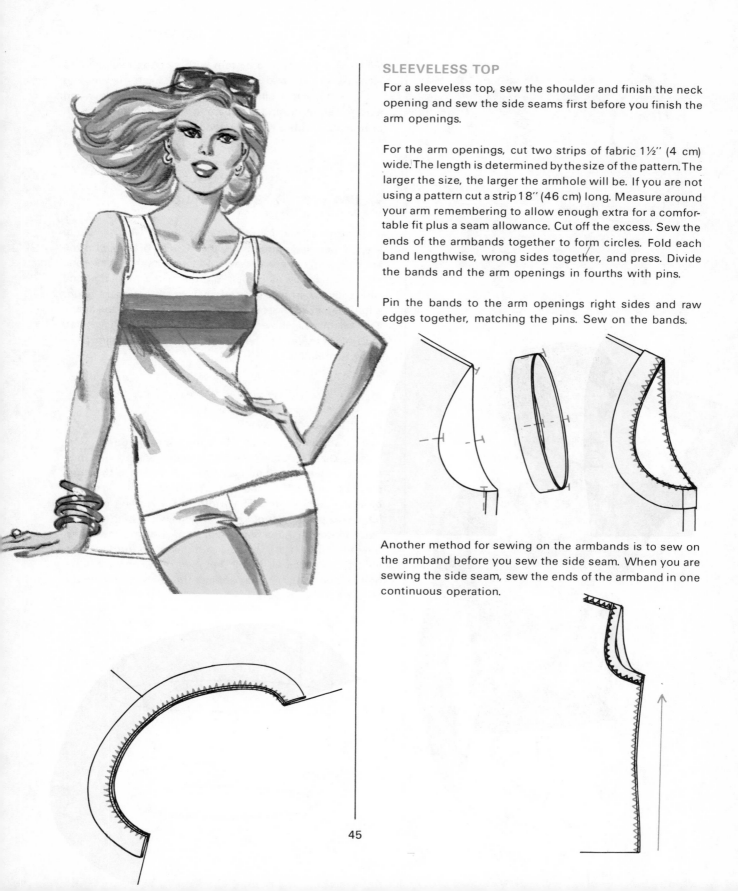

SLEEVELESS TOP

For a sleeveless top, sew the shoulder and finish the neck opening and sew the side seams first before you finish the arm openings.

For the arm openings, cut two strips of fabric 1½'' (4 cm) wide. The length is determined by the size of the pattern. The larger the size, the larger the armhole will be. If you are not using a pattern cut a strip 18'' (46 cm) long. Measure around your arm remembering to allow enough extra for a comfortable fit plus a seam allowance. Cut off the excess. Sew the ends of the armbands together to form circles. Fold each band lengthwise, wrong sides together, and press. Divide the bands and the arm openings in fourths with pins.

Pin the bands to the arm openings right sides and raw edges together, matching the pins. Sew on the bands.

Another method for sewing on the armbands is to sew on the armband before you sew the side seam. When you are sewing the side seam, sew the ends of the armband in one continuous operation.

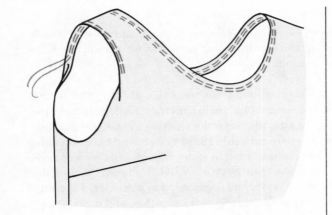

When using a knit top pattern with a scoop neck and no sleeves, an easy and quick method to finish the arm and neck openings is to simply turn the raw edges to the wrong side and stitch around the opening with a decorative stitch or topstitch with a double needle.

VARIATIONS FOR BOTTOM EDGES OF T-SHIRTS AND TOPS

The bottom edge of a knit top can be finished in a number of ways depending upon the style and finish of the fabric you are using. The simplest way is to turn a hem to the wrong side and hem by machine. Fold under the raw edge and sew, using a narrow zigzag stitch. If you are using a straight stitch, you have to stretch the fabric as you sew the seam. This seam will show on the right side. If you want an invisible hem, sew the hem by hand or if your machine has a blind hem stitch, use it.

RIBBING WAISTBAND

A very attractive way to finish the bottom edge is with ribbing. Cut the ribbing across the grain, long enough to fit snugly around you. You may have to use more than one piece of ribbing. If so, the seams joining the ribbing should be at the side seams. The width of the ribbing depends upon your personal preference. Cut the width of the ribbing twice the width of the finished band plus seam allowances. Sew the ends of the waistband together to form a circle. Fold the waistband double lengthwise, wrong sides together, matching the seams. Mark the center front and the center back with pins.

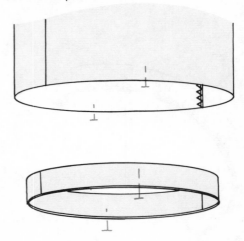

46

Pin the waistband to the bottom edge of the shirt with the right sides and the raw edges together. Match the pins at the center front and the center back. Match the side seams. Sew the waistband to the shirt, stretching the waistband to fit the bottom edge of the shirt.

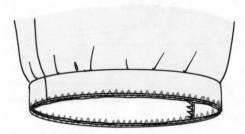

DRAWSTRING

You can obtain an attractive variation by using a drawstring at the bottom. So that you can tie the drawstring, make two buttonholes ½'' (1.3 cm) out from the center front and approximately 1¼'' (3.2 cm) up from the bottom edge. To keep the buttonholes from stretching, you should stabilize the fabric under the buttonholes. Under the buttonholes, pin a piece of woven fabric or interfacing. Make two vertical buttonholes approximately ½'' (1.3 cm) long. Trim the interfacing close to the buttonholes.

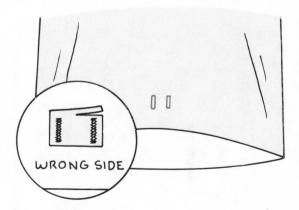

WRONG SIDE

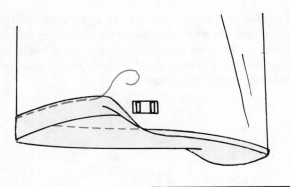

Fold the hem to the wrong side to form a casing 1¼'' (3.2 cm). Turn under the raw edges and sew close to the edge all around the bottom. For the drawstring, cut a strip of fabric on the grain 1¼'' (3.2 cm) wide and long enough to go around you plus enough to make a tie at the center front.

Fold the strip double, right sides together, lengthwise. Sew the drawstring using a narrow seam allowance along the long edge. Turn the strip right side out.

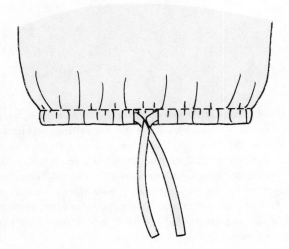

Refer to the top with a front slit for an easy way to turn the drawstring. Insert one end of the drawstring in one buttonhole, thread the drawstring all the way around the bottom and out the other buttonhole.

Instead of a drawstring, you may wish to use elastic in the casing. Eliminate the buttonholes. When you are sewing the casing, leave a 1'' (2.5 cm) opening for inserting the elastic. Cut a piece of elastic long enough to go around you comfortably. Insert the elastic, sew the ends of the elastic together and close the opening.

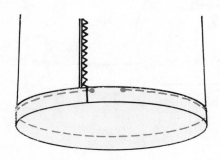

You can also use elastic around the bottom edge of the sleeves. Follow the same procedure as used for the bottom of the shirt. If you are using elastic, it looks more attractive if the sleeve is fuller. To widen the sleeves, draw a line from the bottom edge of the cap to the bottom of the sleeve. Extend the bottom line out for as much fullness as you wish. Be sure to extend the same amount on both sides.

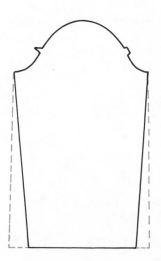

VARIATIONS

There are a great many changes which can be done to a basic T-shirt or knit top in order to give the garment a personal touch. This also applies to a knit dress. Some of the changes do not require any changes in the pattern itself. The addition of a breast pocket, using a contrasting trim around the neck and cuffs, or a pocket near the bottom of a shirt, are only a few of the changes that can easily be made.

STRIPES

By the use of contrasting color, you can achieve some very striking variations. Stripes are easy to apply and you may use them almost anywhere; around the sleeve, down the sleeve, across the front, on the shoulders or down the front.

Apply the stripes before you sew the top together except when the stripes are on the shoulder. In this case, you have to sew the shoulder seam first. To make a stripe cut a strip of fabric long enough to go across the area. The width is determined by your personal preference, however, it should be ½'' (1.3 cm) wider than the finished strip. Fold under the long edges ¼'' (6 mm) to the wrong side and press. Pin the stripe to the shirt at the desired location and sew it on close to the edges. The fabric underneath the stripe can either be left or you can trim it away.

sweaters

A sweater is a garment that everyone uses. The two basic styles are pull-on and cardigan, however, these basic styles can be made with a lot of variations. Sometime ago, sweater fabric was the only fabric used for a sweater, however, many other fabrics have been developed which make excellent sweaters. Some of the fabrics which can be used are stretch velour, stretch terry and other textured knits.

KWIK·SEW has patterns especially designed for sweaters. These patterns are designed for fabric with 35% stretch across the grain. They have less ease and usually have a ¼'' (6mm) seam allowance included. Patterns designed for sweaters usually have simple lines; darts and interfacing are eliminated. The important thing to remember is to check the stretch of the fabric to be sure that the fabric has enough stretch. Use the stretch chart that is included on the envelope or in the catalog.

Sewing on these fabrics is not difficult, however, there are a few techniques which make it easier. Use a ball point needle and polyester thread. A roller presser foot is very helpful when sewing on these fabrics. A roller presser foot will help both layers of these fabrics to feed evenly. The sewing procedure and seams will be the same as used for single knits, but it is helpful to loosen the pressure on the presser foot. If there is excessive pressure on the presser foot, it will stretch out the seams. It is important to keep the presser foot on the fabric and avoid sewing over the edge as this will also stretch out the fabric.

Be sure to press each seam as it is sewn. Always use steam and let the steam do the work for you, just lightly let the iron touch your fabric.

We will start off by giving the techniques for making a sweater using sweater fabric. The techniques are the same for other types of fabric such as velour, stretch terry, etc.

Many people are amazed when they find out that it is possible to construct a beautiful sweater on a sewing machine. The first question they ask is, ''Will the fabric unravel when you cut it?'' The answer is ''No''. This is the same method as used by sweater manufacturers. Because of the way the fabric is knitted, the loops tend to lock into each other when the fabric is cut.

A sweater is one of the fastest and easiest garments you can make. You should be able to complete a beautiful sweater in less than thirty minutes. The reason for this is that most sweater fabric has a finished ribbing which is used for the bottom of the sweater and the cuffs. This eliminates all hemming.

SWEATER FABRICS

Sweater fabric is available in a large variety of fibers, designs and textures. Some fabric is very heavy such as the type used for ski sweaters; some is very light and can be used for a simple lightweight pullover.

There are three basic types of sweater fabric: sweater bodies, sweater blankets and sweater yardage. The yarn can be the same for all three types. The difference is determined by the type of knitting machine on which the fabric was made.

A sweater body, also known as a sweater tube, is circular in shape. There is a "run" which looks like a flaw. This is not a flaw and it is where you should cut the fabric open before you proceed to cut out the pattern. If you do not do this, the run might appear in the sweater.

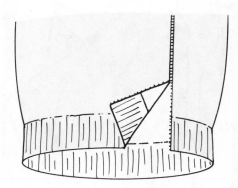

A sweater blanket comes already cut open. One edge of both the sweater body and the blanket is finished with ribbing. This ribbing is for the bottom of the sweater and the bottom of the sleeves.

Sweater bodies and blankets come in a great variety of sizes. Make sure when you purchase the sweater fabric that it is large enough for the pattern. Check both the length and the width. Bear in mind that a set-in sleeve requires a shorter piece of fabric than a raglan sleeve.

Some stores carry very large sweater bodies or blankets, and you can usually construct an entire garment from one piece of fabric. However, the most common sweater bodies and blankets are not this large and you have to purchase two bodies or blankets for each garment. Usually you have to cut out a sleeve and the front from one piece and a sleeve and the back from the other piece.

Remember, when you are cutting out a raglan sleeve that you need a left and right sleeve, as the back shoulder seam is longer than the front shoulder seam. Both sleeves are the same on a set-in sleeve sweater. Some stores carry two sizes of sweater bodies made from the same fabric. The large body is used for the front and back; the small body is used for the sleeves.

You can also find sweater fabric in the form of yardage.

When you use sweater yardage, you have to hem the sleeves and the bottom of the sweater, or you can sew on special cuffs or finish the bottom with special trim.

Stores which carry sweater fabric usually carry ribbing which is used around the neck opening. This ribbing may also be used for cuffs. If you cannot obtain ribbing you can always use self-fabric cut across the grain so that the most stretch goes lengthwise. This is important. If you do not do this, the neckline will not stretch enough to go over your head. This can be overcome by putting a zipper in the back. Even when using ribbing some women prefer to use a zipper so that their hair will not be disarranged when pulling the garment over their head.

CUTTING

Before you cut out the fabric, check the measurements with the pattern so that you are sure you obtain the correct length for the body and the sleeves.

If you are using a sweater body or a blanket with tight ribbing at the bottom edge, be sure to stretch out the ribbing so the rib of the fabric is straight with the rib on the ribbing. Hold the stretched ribbing in place with tape, or if you are cutting out the fabric on a cutting board, you can pin the fabric to the cutting board.

To obtain a ribbed finish on the bottom of the sweater and the sleeves, place the bottom of the pattern pieces, edge to edge, with the bottom of the ribbing.

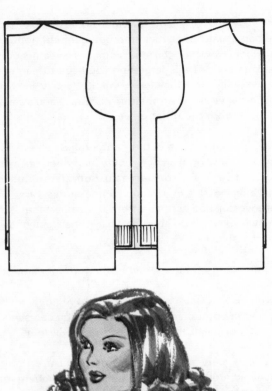

If you are constructing a sweater and the fabric piece is not quite long enough for the pattern, place the shoulder of the back and front pattern pieces as near the top raw edge of the fabric as possible so that the bottom fo the sweater will have a finished edge. The front and back of the sweater will now be shorter than the pattern pieces. This is usually acceptable for the body, however, it will not work for the sleeves. Therefore, if you do not have sufficient length for the sleeves, we suggest that you make short sleeves. If you want short sleeves, indicate the length of the sleeve on the pattern piece. Place this mark on the bottom of the ribbing so that the short sleeve will have a finished edge. The sleeve will probably be too wide so you will have to reduce the width.

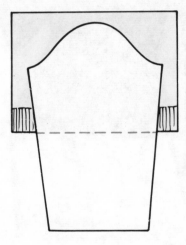

If the sweater fabric has a textured design or a color design either throughout the fabric or only on parts of the fabric, you have to be more careful when you cut out the pattern so that the design matches at the seam.

If the fabric has a design, measure the sleeve length first and cut out the sleeves. Measure the distance from the design to the underarm point; line up the back and front pattern pieces so that the distance from the design to the underarm point is exactly the same; then cut out the back and the front pieces.

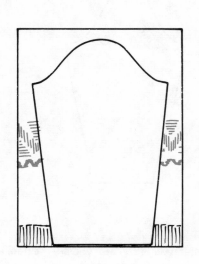 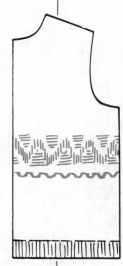 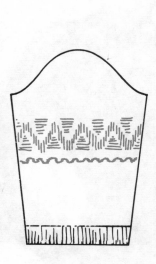 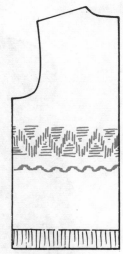

If you are using very loosely knitted fabric, we suggest that after you have cut out the pattern pieces that you shake the fabric and then match the pattern piece to the fabric, You may find that as a result of the shaking, the fabric has stretched. This is especially true of the sleeves. Trim off the excess fabric at the top. It is a good idea to do this for all sweater fabric regardless of how loosely it is knitted.

If you are using sweater yardage which does not have a finished ribbing on the bottom, check your measurements with the pattern for the correct length of the body and the sleeves. The sleeves and the body of the sweater can be finished with a hem or you can add a band and cuffs. If you are using a light to medium weight fabric, you can use the same fabric for the band on the bottom edge and the sleeve cuffs. If the fabric is heavy, we recommend using ribbing. Take into consideration the fact that the width of the ribbing you plan to use at the bottom of the sweater and sleeves will lengthen the sweater and the sleeves by an amount equal to the width of the ribbing.

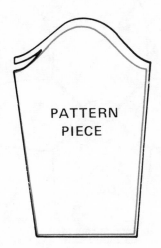

PATTERN PIECE

When cutting out a raglan sleeve sweater, we suggest that you mark the front and back shoulder seams, as they are not identical and it is easy to sew them incorrectly. Place a piece of transparent tape on the wrong side and mark with a pencil on the tape on the front and back shoulder seams.

PULLOVER

Regardless of what type of sweater you are making, a set-in sleeve or a raglan sleeve, the first step is to sew the shoulder seams. The sweater should look like the diagram.

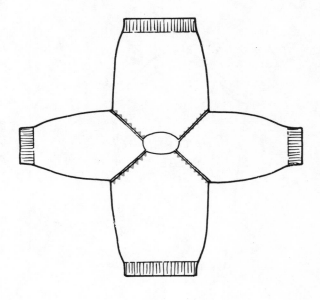

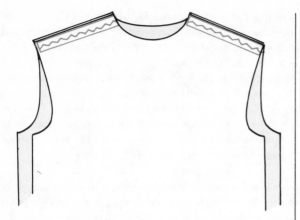

To eliminate stretching of the shoulder seams on a set-in sleeve sweater, you can sew a non-stretch seam binding to the shoulder seams. Cut a piece of seam binding the length of the shoulder. Use the pattern piece to measure, not the cut out garment.

Pin the front to the back, right sides together. Place the seam binding at the front shoulder seam and sew the shoulder seam through all layers. Press the shoulder seam toward the back.

If you are using sweater fabric, you can sometimes use the threads from the fabric if they are easy to unravel and are strong enough. Unravel three or four threads from the fabric; stretch these threads, then steam press them. When you sew the shoulder seams, place these threads under the presser foot and sew them into the seams. You can obtain the same effect by using regular yarn or thread.

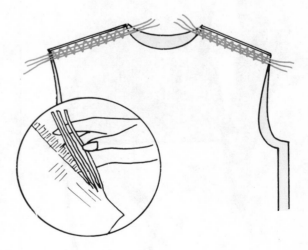

The next step is to finish the neck opening. Various types of neck openings may be used and which type you choose depends upon your personal preference.

For a regular round neck and a V-neck, refer to Section II as the construction is the same.

You use the same procedures for a turtleneck or a mock turtleneck as used for the round neck; the only difference is the width of the neckband. The most common width for a mock turtle neckband is 4½″ (11 cm). The width of a turtleneck depends upon how many times you wish to fold it. If the band has a finished edge, you can use a single thickness of band. This will be approximately 5½″ (14 cm) wide. If the band does not have a finished edge, we suggest that you make the neckband using a double thickness of fabric and the width should be 9½″ (24 cm).

If you are using a piece of flat ribbing with one finished edge for the turtleneck and you plan to have a neckband with one layer of fabric, you have to sew the seam in a special way so that the seam will not show when the turtleneck is folded over. When sewing the ends of the band together, be sure that the part of the band going towards the neck opening is sewn on the wrong side 2″ (5 cm) up from the raw edges.

Turn the collar inside out and sew the rest ot the seam on the opposite side of the fabric. Now when you turn over the turtleneck collar, no raw edges will show.

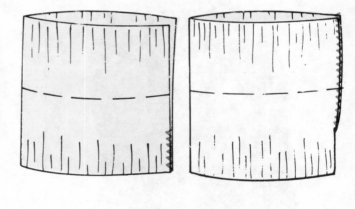

If you are constructing a sweater with a set-in sleeve, match the center top of the sleeve with the shoulder seam, right side to right side. The front and the back of these sleeves are identical so either one may be used as the left or right sleeve.

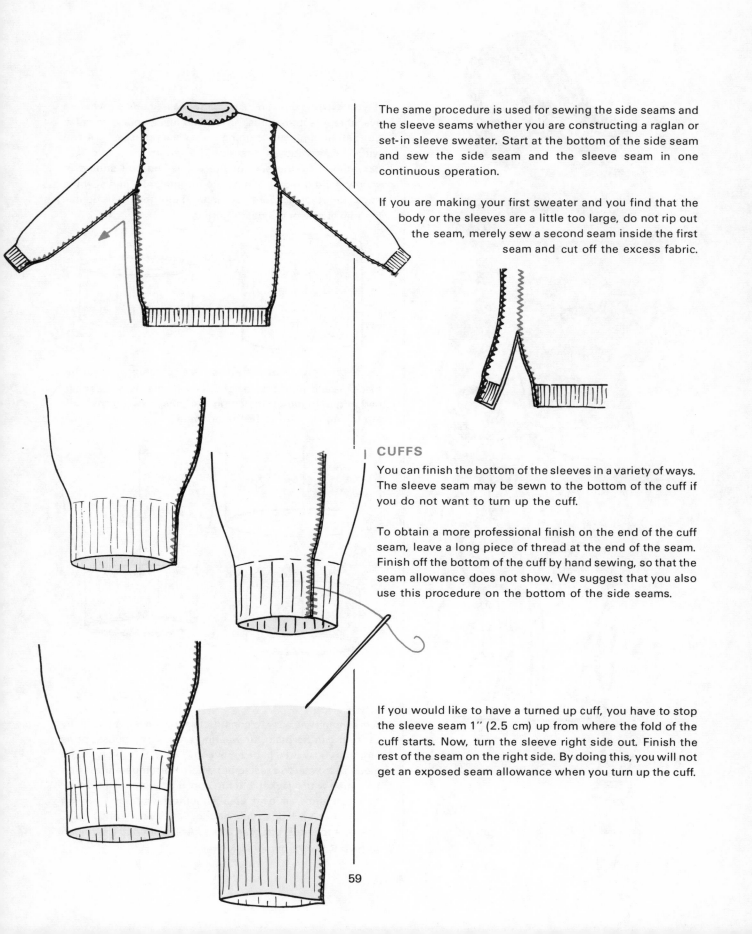

The same procedure is used for sewing the side seams and the sleeve seams whether you are constructing a raglan or set-in sleeve sweater. Start at the bottom of the side seam and sew the side seam and the sleeve seam in one continuous operation.

If you are making your first sweater and you find that the body or the sleeves are a little too large, do not rip out the seam, merely sew a second seam inside the first seam and cut off the excess fabric.

CUFFS

You can finish the bottom of the sleeves in a variety of ways. The sleeve seam may be sewn to the bottom of the cuff if you do not want to turn up the cuff.

To obtain a more professional finish on the end of the cuff seam, leave a long piece of thread at the end of the seam. Finish off the bottom of the cuff by hand sewing, so that the seam allowance does not show. We suggest that you also use this procedure on the bottom of the side seams.

If you would like to have a turned up cuff, you have to stop the sleeve seam 1″ (2.5 cm) up from where the fold of the cuff starts. Now, turn the sleeve right side out. Finish the rest of the seam on the right side. By doing this, you will not get an exposed seam allowance when you turn up the cuff.

59

If you wish, you can use ready-make cuffs which are available in some stores, or you can make your own cuffs. Cut a straight piece of ribbing across the grain 5½″ (14 cm) wide, or as wide as desired. The length of the cuff is determined by the size of the wrist. The cuff should fit snugly. Fold the strip, right side to right side, and sew the ends together to form a circle. Fold the cuff double lengthwise, wrong sides together.

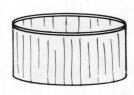

Using pins, divide the cuff and sleeve openings into fourths. Place the cuff, right side to right side with the sleeve opening, raw edges together, matching the pins. Sew on the cuff, stretching the cuff to fit the opening.

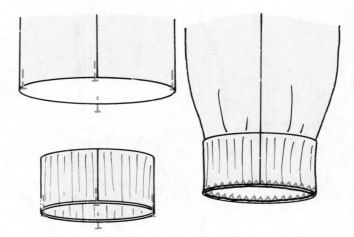

CARDIGAN

A cardigan is as easy to construct as a pullover. It has many uses--It can be plain for wearing around the house, or as fancy as you want it to be for evening wear. It is a very useful garment to wear to a restaurant where the temperature is fine for a man with a jacket, but too cool for a woman in a dress. You can throw it over your shoulders without worrying about what it will do to your hairdo. Fancy yarn work, beads, pearls, appliques, etc., can all be easily added to a cardigan to give it a very personal look.

Not only are sweaters easy and fast to construct but because of the stretch factor in the fabric, it is very easy to change a simple pullover pattern into a cardigan. You merely add to the center front 1'' (2.5 cm). This applies if you are using grosgrain ribbon at the center front. If you plan to finish the center front with self-fabric, you only add the seam allowance. When cutting out the front, cut the center front open. For a round neck, cut all the way up to the neckline. If you wish to construct a cardigan with a V-neck, you simply cut the neckline following the lines indicated on the pullover pattern. If the V-neck is not indicated on your pattern, lower the center front 5½'' (14 cm) and cut as illustrated.

If you would like to construct a cardigan or a vest without side seams, it is very easy to adjust the patterns. Place the back and the front pattern pieces on a flat surface. Overlap the side seam allowances at the arm opening ¼'' (6 mm). Move the pattern pieces so that the outside (center front and center back) lines are parallel. Place a piece of paper underneath the slit at the side seams. Tape the side seams in place. Now you have only one pattern piece. the reason many women do not want side seams is so that they do not have to match a pattern design on the fabric which sometimes can be very difficult, especially if you are using a fabric with a striped design. You can only eliminate side seams when you are using a pattern with an open front.

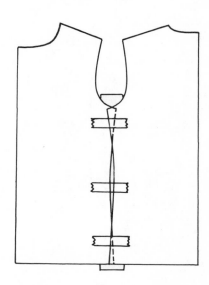

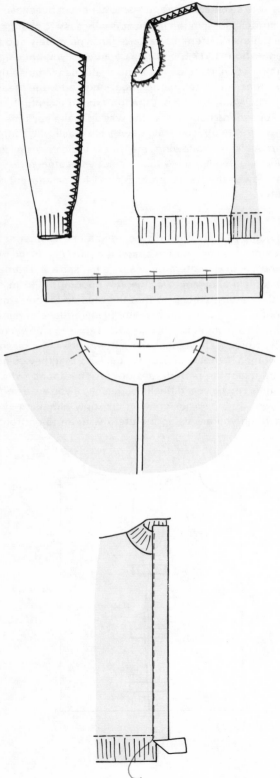

When you are constructing a cardigan, start by sewing the shoulder seams, sew in the sleeves and then the side seams. This is done in the same manner as used for the pullover. If you have cut out a cardigan without a side seam, you sew the shoulder seam, the sleeve seams and then sew in the sleeves.

ROUND NECK CARDIGAN

For the neckband on a round neck cardigan, cut a straight piece of fabric or ribbing across the grain 2'' (5 cm) wide. You can make the neckband wider if you desire. As the stretch factor varies in different types of ribbing or fabric, you have to be sure to cut a long enough strip. A 16'' (40 cm) strip should be long enough.

To get the correct size for the neckband, stretch the band around your neck so that it feels comfortable. Cut off the excess fabric.

Fold and press the neckband double lengthwise with the wrong sides together. Divide the neckband and the neck opening into fourths with pins. Pin the band to the right side of the neck opening with the raw edges together. Match the pins and front edges and sew on the band. You have to stretch the band as you sew so that it will fit the neck opening.

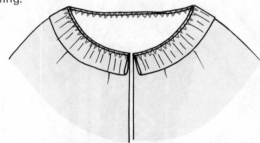

The most common method of finishing the front of a lady's cardigan is with a strip of grosgrain ribbon. We recommend that you preshrink the ribbon before you use it. Cut two lengths of 1'' (2.5 cm) grosgrain ribbon long enough for the front plus 1'' (2.5 cm).

Overlap the ribbon on the right side of each front ¼'' (6 mm), ½'' (1.3 cm) should extend on the top and the bottom. Sew on the ribbon close to the inner edge with a straight stitch.

62

Turn the ribbon to the wrong side. The buttons and buttonholes will hold the ribbon in place. Turn the bottom and top ends of the ribbon under and finish with a few hand stitches.

You may want to use the grosgrain ribbon as a decorative strip on the front of the sweater. If so, overlap the ribbon on the wrong side of each front. Sew it on and turn the ribbon to the right side. Finish the top and the bottom using the same method as you used when the ribbon was placed on the wrong side. Topstitch close to the other edge of the ribbon.

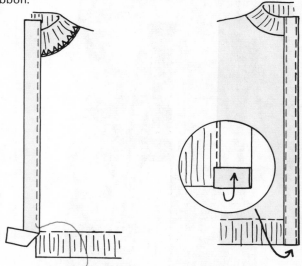

If you wish you may finish the front of the cardigan using sweater fabric. Cut two straight pieces of fabric either along or across the grain. The length of each piece of fabric should be the same as the length of the front opening plus ½'' (1.3 cm). The width of the strips should be approximately 2½'' (6 cm). Fold the bands lengthwise with the wrong sides together. Press the bands. After pressing you should check the length of the bands as the pressing may have slightly stretched them. If this has occurred, cut off the excess fabric.

At the ends of each band, fold the bands, right side to right side, and sew across. Turn right side out. Place the bands on the right side of the cardigan, raw edges together. Be sure that the edges are even with the neck opening and the bottom edge. Sew on the band.

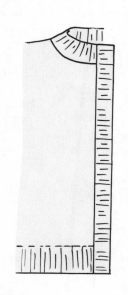

V-NECK CARDIGAN

The advantage of a V-neck cardigan is that you can extend the length of the body to give you the appearance of a jacket. A couple of pockets placed near the bottom of the sweater will also add to the jacket appearance. A few minor adjustments may have to be made in the pattern.

The front and neck openings may be finished using different types of trimmings; these are usually flat trim, ribbing or self-fabric.

KWIK·SEW patterns come with special pattern pieces for the front and neck opening.

If you are using patterns which do not give you the length of the trim going around the neck and front opening, measure the pattern piece, not the cut out fabric. The band should be approximately 1½'' (3.8 cm) smaller than the back of the neck opening and ½'' (1.3 cm) smaller from the shoulder to the first buttonhole. Add ¼'' (6 mm) on each end to be used for the bottom seam allowance.

If you do not have special trim and you want to use self fabric, it may be cut either across or with the grain. It should be approximately 2½'' (6 cm) wide.

Start by finishing the bottom edges of the band. Fold the ends of the band, right side to right side. Sew across using ¼'' (6 mm) which is the seam allowance for each edge at the bottom front. Turn right side out.

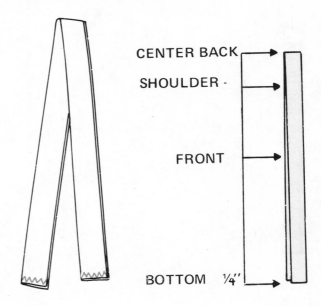

CENTER BACK

SHOULDER

FRONT

BOTTOM ¼''

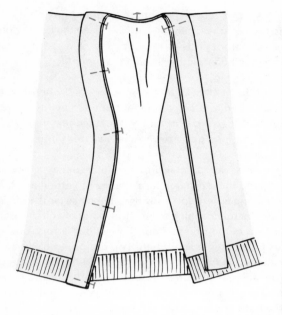

Fold the band double, lengthwise, wrong side to wrong side, and press. Pin the band to the front and neck opening with the raw edges and the right sides together. Match the center back, mark for the shoulder seams and the bottom of the neckline. Place the ends of the bands even with the bottom of the sweater. Sew on the band, stretching it to fit the cardigan.

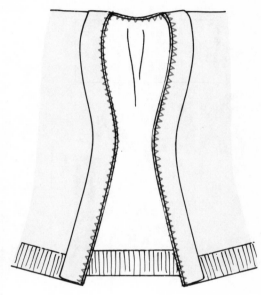

BUTTONS AND BUTTONHOLES

To determine where to place the buttonholes regardless of the style of the sweater, always remember that the first buttonhole should be placed over the highest point of the bust. This is to eliminate the possibility of a gap. From this point, you place the other buttonholes an equal distance apart.

On a round neck cardigan, the top buttonhole is horizontal on the neckband and other buttonholes are vertical. The buttonholes should be placed in the middle of the grosgrain ribbon. On a V-neck cardigan, all the buttonholes are placed in a vertical position. When you are using ribbing or self-fabric for the front trim, place the buttonholes in the center of the trim.

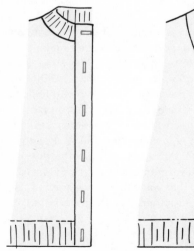

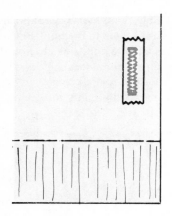

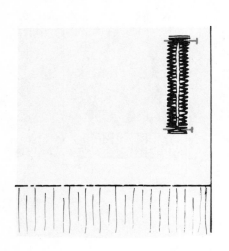

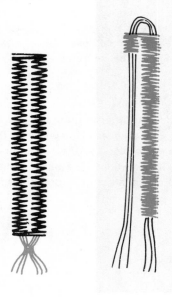

When making a lady's garment, everything goes from the right to the left side. Therefore, always place the buttonholes on the right front. This is the opposite of where they are placed when constructing a man's garment.

It is very difficult to make buttonholes by hand when sewing on sweater fabric. It can be done, but you have to be very careful; for if you do not sew the stitches very close together, you may get a run in the sweater fabric.

It is much easier to make buttonholes using a sewing machine and there is much less chance of getting a run. As sweater fabric is very soft and sometimes has large loops, it is difficult for the machine to feed the material and the loops often catch in the presser foot. To overcome this, place a strip of transparent tape where you are going to sew the buttonhole. Use the type of tape you can write on. Mark the position and size of the buttonhole with a pencil. Use slightly longer stitches than when sewing regular fabric. Sew the buttonhole through the tape; then remove the tape when the buttonhole is completed.

When you cut open the buttonholes, it is a good idea to place a pin at the end of the buttonhole at cross angles to the buttonhole. This will prevent you from cutting too large a hole and perhaps ruining your garment.

After you remove the tape, you may find that there are small pieces which are difficult to remove. You can remove these pieces by using a steam iron. Do not touch the garment with the iron. The heat from the steam will cause the small pieces of tape to curl up and they can then be brushed off.

A corded buttonhole is stronger and much more attractive than a regular buttonhole. You can use regular buttonhole cording, buttonhole twist, or take a few strands of fabric, depending upon how heavy the fabric is. Stretch these strands and steam press them to remove the kinks. Place the cording strands under the presser foot and then sew the buttonhole. Refer to your sewing machine instruction book for more details on how this is done on your particular type of sewing machine. Always start from the bottom of the buttonhole and leave enough cording or yarn where you start and finish, so that you can pull the ends to the wrong side and tie them together. Cut off the excess.

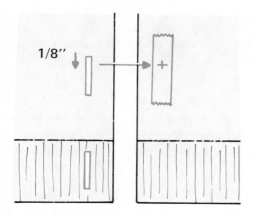

Buttons can be sewn on either by hand or by machine. If you are using a sewing machine, we suggest that you place transparent tape where you are going to sew on the button. The tape prevents this soft fabric from pulling up into the holes in the buttons. Mark the position of the button. It should be ⅛'' (2 mm) down from the top of the buttonhole. Drop the feed dogs; set the machine for zigzag. The width of the stitch should be the same as the distance between the holes in the buttons. Again refer to your sewing machine instruction book.

POCKETS

You can have one breast pocket, two breast pockets, one side pocket, two side pockets or you can have all four pockets on a sweater if you desire. They are very easy to make.

If you have some sweater fabric left over which has one finished edge, use the edge for the top of the pocket. Cut out the size of pocket you wish to have. Overcast the three raw edges. Fold the raw edges under ½'' (1.3 cm) and press.

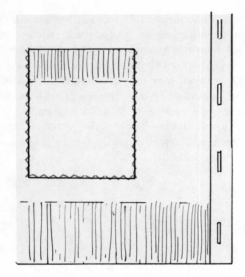

Pin the pocket at the desired location. Sew on the pocket around the three sides using a very narrow zigzag stitch. Try to make sure that every other stitch catches the pocket.

If you wish you may topstitch a little distance in from the edge of the pocket. This will give the pocket a different appearance. Here again use a very narrow zigzag stitch.

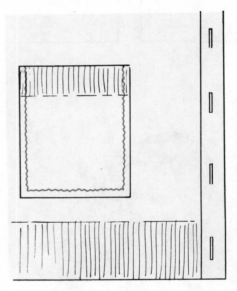

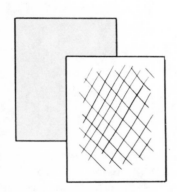

If you wish to have pockets and do not have any fabric with a finished edge, cut out the pocket in sweater fabric with four raw edges. Cut the same size pocket out of lining fabric.

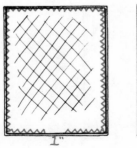

Place the lining, right side to right side, with the pocket. Sew around the pocket leaving an opening 1'' (2.5 cm). Turn the pocket right side out. Close the opening with a few stitches by hand.

Topstitch across the top of the pocket ¼'' (6 mm) in from the edge. Sew on the pocket using a very narrow zigzag stitch.

68

SWEATER DRESSES

When you are constructing a dress using either sweater fabric, velour or stretch terry, the sewing techniques are the same as described for sewing sweaters. It is sometimes difficult to hem garments made from velour and stretch terry. The easiest way is to use fusible webbing. This will help eliminate the hem stretching and puckering.

Before hemming, it is best to let the dress hang overnight so that the fabric will take its natural shape.

In addition to a regular pattern, with a few changes, you can also use a pattern for a pullover sweater. You have to extend the length. The simplest way to do this is to place the back and the front of the sweater pattern on a flat surface with the side seams facing each other. Leave a space between the pattern pieces equal to 4'' (10 cm). Place a large piece of paper underneath the bottom edge of the pattern. The paper should be as long as you wish the finished dress to be. Tape the pattern pieces to this paper. Using a straight edge ruler, extend the center front and the center back line all the way down to the bottom edge of the paper.

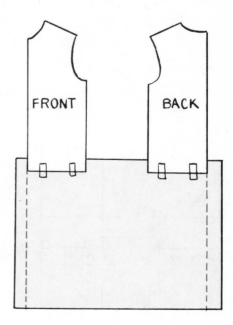

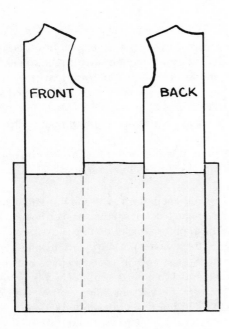

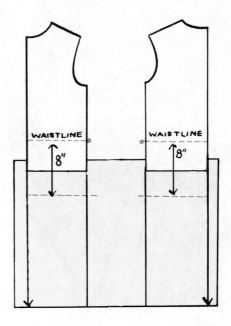

Extend the back and front sides to the bottom of the paper.

Now measure your own back length from the neck to the waist. Mark the pattern piece where the waistline will be. From the waistline measure down 8″ (20 cm). Take your own hip measurement. Divide this measurement in half. Measure from the hip point at the center front and the center back towards the sides. If your hip measurement is larger than the pattern, divide the difference in half and add this amount to each side.

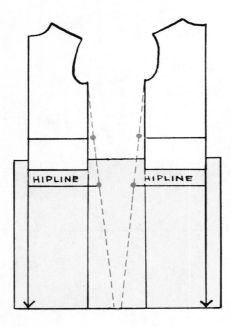

Now with a ruler, draw a line from the arm opening through the hip point all the way down to the bottom of the dress. Do this on both the back and front sides.

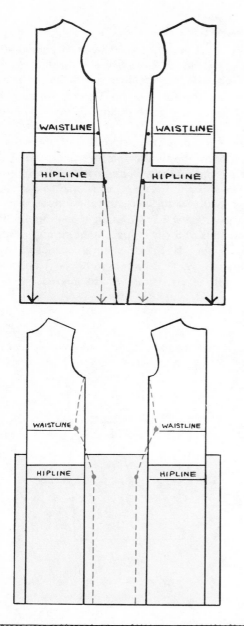

If you usually require a larger size pattern for the skirt than you do for the top, the line from the hip to the bottom of the skirt should be adjusted. Make a straight line from the hip point down to the bottom of the side.

If you would prefer a more form fitted dress, draw the line from the bottom of the arm opening to the waist approximately as illustrated. Join the points at the waist and the hip with a curved line.

The belt for a dress made from stretch fabric can be either a ready-made belt or you can make a tie belt. Cut a strip of fabric 1¼ yard (1.15 m) long, 2″ (5 cm) wide. Fold the strip double, right sides together lengthwise. The ends of the belt can either be sewn straight across or at an angle. Sew the belt using a narrow seam allowance along all the raw edges. Be sure to leave a 1″ (2.5 cm) opening at the center of the belt. Turn the belt right side out through the opening.

An easy way to turn a belt right side out is to use a pen or a pencil. Tuck the sewn end in and using the pen or pencil, push in to turn the belt right side out.

Close the opening by sewing a few stitches by hand.

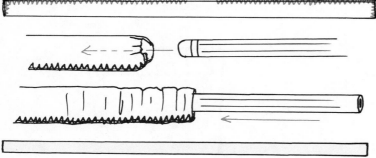

STRIPE INSERTS

Very attractive effects can be achieved by adding stripes from contrasting fabric. These are especially attractive on tops made with velour or stretch terry. Stripes can be added to sleeves, the shoulders or the fronts. The number of stripes and the location depends upon personal preference.

Decide how wide you want the stripes and where they will be located. Mark the pattern pieces where they will be placed. When you cut out the pattern pieces for the stripes, you have to allow for seam allowances. You add seam allowances to the width you want the stripes. This also applies to the regular pattern piece. For example, if you wish to make a 1'' (2.5 cm) stripe, cut the strip 1½'' (3.8 cm) wide, allowing for ¼'' (6 mm) seam allowances. Cut away from the pattern ½'' (1.3 cm). If you do not do this, the length or width of the pattern will be altered.

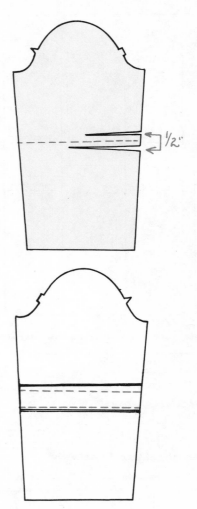

blouses and shirts

Both blouses and shirts are constructed using lightweight fabric. It can be either stretch or non-stretch fabric; the construction is the same. You can have an almost endless number of styles for both of these garments. We will just discuss the basic styles. We recommend that you use interfacing for the collar, front facing and on the cuffs if you plan to use them. When using a one-piece cuff, extend the interfacing ½" (1.3 cm) beyond the folding line. The easiest interfacing to use is the press-on type.

Some fabrics do not lend themselves well to press-on interfacing. They will have that "glued" look which is not attractive. Always try the type of interfacing you plan to use on a scrap of the same fabric to see if you will be pleased with the results. If you do not wish to use press-on interfacing, choose a crisp but not heavy interfacing for the shirt.

The easiest way to use interfacing for small pieces is to fuse the fabric onto the interfacing before you cut out the pieces. When using press-on interfacing, place the side that contains the glue on the wrong side of the fabric. Use a steam iron to fuse the fabric to the interfacing. Make sure you use an up and down motion to eliminate the possibility of stretching the fabric out of shape.

If you get any of the interfacing glue on your ironing board, the best way to remove it is to iron on a brown paper bag. This will remove the glue.

After you have cut out the pattern pieces, press on the interfacing. For the front facing, it is easier to obtain a straight line if you first press the folding line at the front. This makes it easier to place the interfacing so that it is exactly straight.

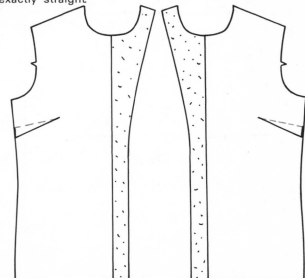

Sew the front darts and the shoulder seams.

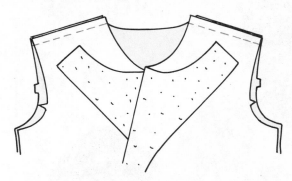

Pin the upper and the under collar, right sides together, and stitch the outer edge and the ends. At the corners shorten the stitch length and, if the collar has a sharp point, make one stitch across the point.

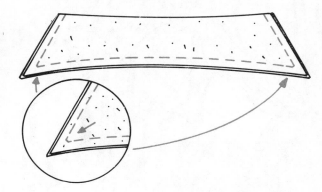

Collars will always look professionally made if the collar is pressed before turning and all the seam allowances are pressed open on a point presser.

If necessary, grade the seam allowances, trim the corners, turn right side out. Press the collar, rolling the outer seam slightly toward the under collar side. Topstitch the collar ¼'' (6 mm) from the finished edge.

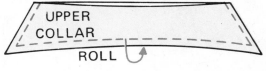

UPPER COLLAR

ROLL

UNDER COLLAR

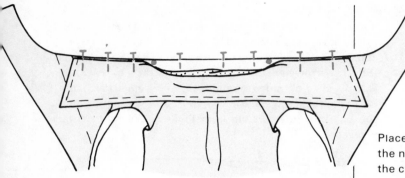

Place the right side of the under collar to the right side of the neck opening, matching the center back of the collar to the center back of the neck opening. The ends of the collar should be at the center front.

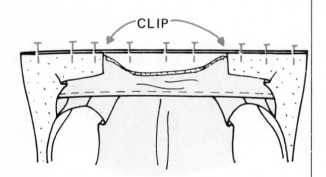

CLIP

Fold the front facing on the folding line to the right side over the collar. Pin the facing to the collar and neckline through all layers. Clip the seam allowance on the upper collar at the end of the facing. Sew on the collar by sewing through all layers the width of the facing. Continue sewing only the under collar to the neckline and again sew through all layers the width of the facing on the other side. Turn the facing to the inside.

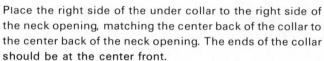

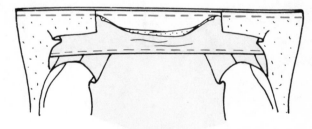

Clip the seam allowance at the end of the facing. Press the seam allowance into the collar. Fold under the seam allowance on the upper collar. Topstitch close to the fold, or sew in place by hand. Attach the facing to the shoulder seams. Sew the side seams.

CLIP

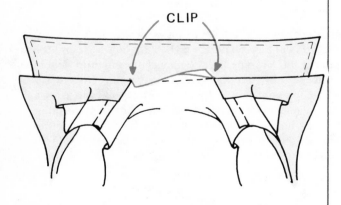

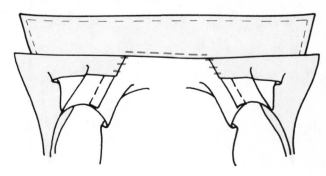

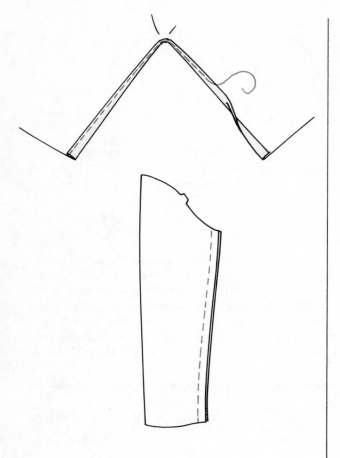

SLEEVE SLITS

If you plan to have long sleeves with cuffs, it is necessary for you to have a slit at the cuff. Cut the slit. There are several different ways of finishing the sleeve slit. The easiest way is to fold a narrow hem to the wrong side and sew by machine. Fold the slit, right sides together, and sew a small dart at the top of the slit. If you are using woven fabric, we suggest that you use a narrow double hem to keep the fabric from unraveling.

Sew the sleeve seam. On the front of the sleeve, fold the edge of the slit ½" (1.3 cm) to the wrong side. Sew across to keep it in place.

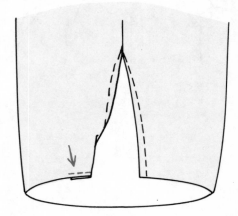

Another easy way to finish the slit when you are using knit fabric is to cut a piece of fabric 1¼" (3.2 cm) wide and the length of the slit plus ½" (1.3 cm). Fold the strip double lengthwise with the wrong sides together. Pin the slit facing to the right side of the slit. Sew from one end using a ⅛" (3 mm) seam allowance. Sew ⅛" (3 mm) past the point of the slit, lower the needle, turn the fabric and sew the other side. Fold the facing, right side to right side, and sew across the top of the facing at an angle.

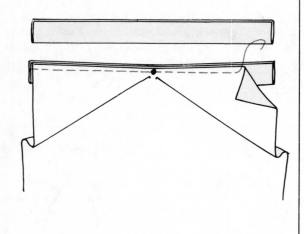

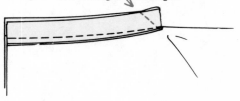

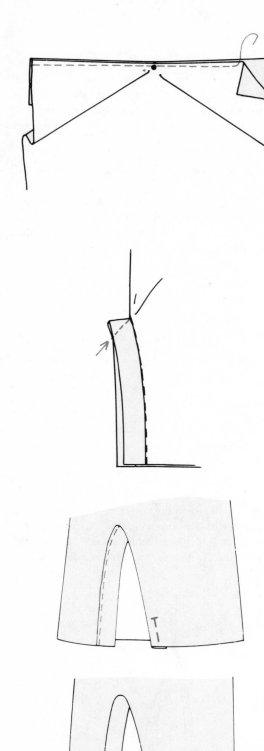

Another method is to cut a piece of fabric 1½″ (3.8 cm) wide and the length of the slit plus ½″ (1.3 cm). Pin the right side of the sleeve slit facing to the wrong side of the slit opening. Stitch from one end using ⅛″ (3 mm) seam allowance. Stitch ⅛″ (3 mm) past the point of the slit, lower the needle, turn the fabric and stitch the other side. Press the seam allowance toward the facing. On the other side of the slit facing, fold the raw edges ¼″ (6 mm) to the wrong side and press. Fold the facing to the right side to cover the stitches and topstitch close to the folded edge.

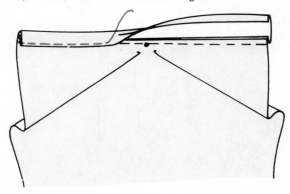

Fold the facing, right side to right side, and stitch across the top of the facing at an angle as illustrated.

Sew the sleeve seam.

Fold the slit facing to the wrong side on the sleeve front (larger part of sleeve). The slit facing extends on the back part of the sleeve.

Sew gathering stitches on the bottom edge of the sleeve or form pleats by pinning fabric, right side to right side, between markings. Pin the pleats toward the slit opening.

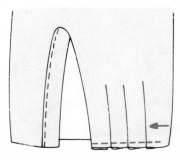

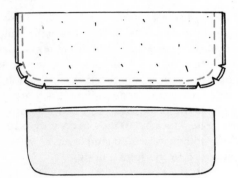

CUFFS

Pin the cuffs, right sides together. Stitch the three sides, leaving the top edge open. Clip the curved seam allowance. Turn the cuffs right side out and press. Pin the interfaced side of the cuff to the bottom edge of the sleeve, right sides and raw edges together.

Sew on the cuff. Press the seam allowance into the cuff.

On the inside, fold under the cuff seam allowance and pin so that it covers the stitches. Sew close to the fold or if you prefer, you can stitch in the ditch on the right side. Topstitch the cuffs.

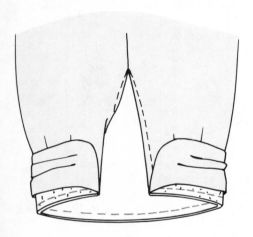
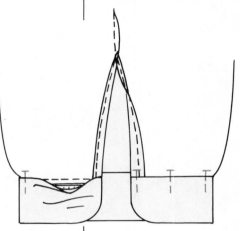
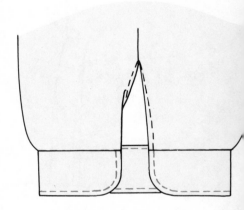

A fast and easy way to attach the cuff is to pin the cuff to the sleeve, right sides and raw edges together. On front part of sleeve, fold ½" (1.3 cm) to right side over cuff. Sew on the cuff through all layers. Overcast the seam allowances. Turn facing to inside.

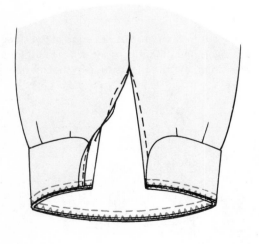
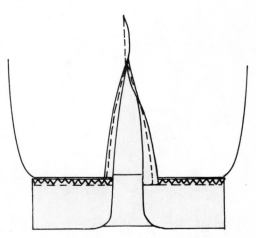

SLEEVES

To ease in extra fullness on the sleeve cap, sew gathering stitches on the cap of the sleeve.

Pin the sleeve to the arm opening, right sides together, matching the notch on the cap of the sleeve to the shoulder seam and the sleeve seam to the side seam. Distribute the ease evenly on the top part of the sleeve. Sew in place.

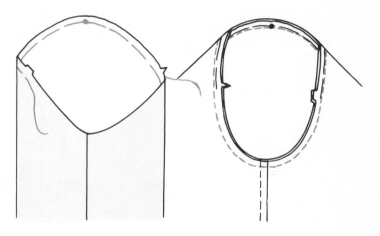

BOTTOM EDGE

Attach the bottom edge of the facing by turning the facing right side to right side on the folding line. Sew a straight seam across the facing at the desired hemline. Turn the facing to the wrong side and hem the bottom edge of the shirt either by hand or by machine.

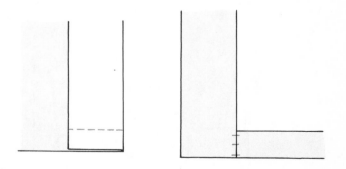

SLEEVELESS BLOUSE

All the construction for a sleeveless blouse is the same as that used on a blouse with sleeves except for the arm opening. If you are using a pattern for a blouse with sleeves, you have to raise the arm opening.

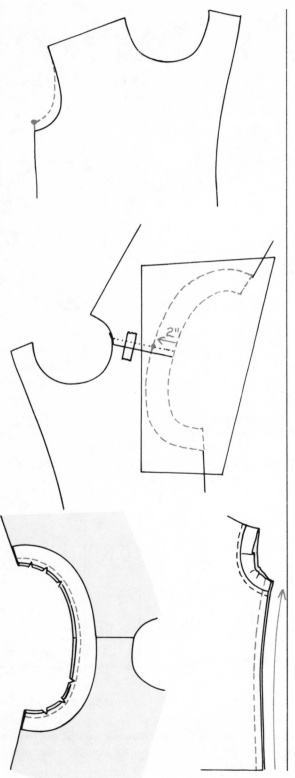

On the front and the back of the pattern piece, raise the arm opening ⅝" (1.5 cm) from the side seams. Draw a smooth connecting line from the shoulder to the raised arm opening.

The arm opening can be finished with a facing, self fabric binding or a strip of fabric to resemble piping.

ARM OPENING WITH FACING

If you do not have a seperate facing piece, you can easily make one. Place the front and back pattern pieces together at the shoulder seam overlapping the seam allowances. From the outer edge of the arm opening, measure in 2" (5 cm) and mark. Draw a curved line this distance in using the same curve as the arm opening. Trace the facing piece on a piece of paper. Cut out the facing.

After you have sewn the shoulder seam and before you have sewn the side seams, place the facing right side to right side with the arm opening. Sew on the facing and trim the seam allowance. Sew the side seam and the facing in one operation. Fold the facing to the wrong side. Attach the facing with a few stitches by hand at the shoulder seam and the side seam. An easy way to attach the facing at the shoulder and the side seam is to sew in the previous seamline on the right side.

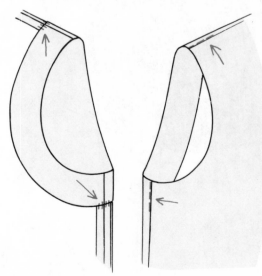

80

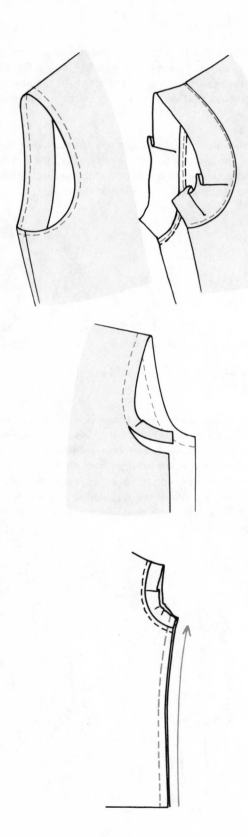

If you have topstitched the collar and the center front, you should use the same topstitching around the arm opening. If you do not topstitch, we suggest that you understitch the facing to prevent it from rolling to the outside. This has to be done before you sew the side seam. To understitch, press the seam allowance towards the facing, sew a seam on the facing close to the seamline through the facing and seam allowances.

SELF FABRIC BINDING

An easy way to finish the arm opening is by binding the raw edges with self fabric. It works especially well on knit fabric and the bulky facings are eliminated.

Trim off the seam allowance on the arm opening. The binding is applied before sewing the side seams.

Cut a piece of fabric for the binding 1½" (3.8 cm) wide and as long as the arm opening, with the stretch going lengthwise. Pin the binding to the arm opening, right sides and raw edges together, and sew using a ¼" (6 mm) seam allowance. Press the seam allowance towards the binding.

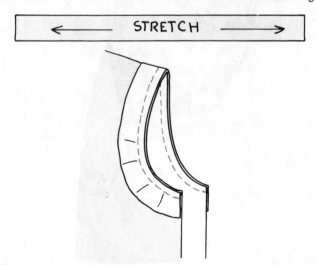

Pin the front to the back at the side seams. Sew the side seam from the bottom edge of the blouse to the outer edge of the binding.

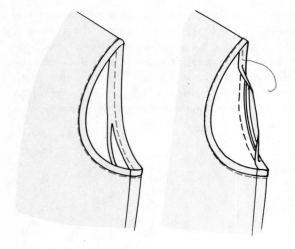

Fold the binding over the seam allowance to the wrong side. The binding will extend beyond the seam. On the outside of the blouse, stitch in the ditch to secure the binding on the inside. Trim the binding on the inside close to the stitches.

If you would like to bind the edges of a blouse made from woven fabric, the binding should be cut on the bias and the edges should be folded under before stitching in the ditch to secure the binding on the inside of the blouse.

BINDING TO RESEMBLE PIPING

For this finish, you can use self fabric or contrasting fabric.

Cut a strip of fabric ⅞'' (2.2 cm) wide and the length of the arm opening.

Fold the strip double lengthwise, wrong sides together, and press. Place the strip on the right side of the arm opening. with the raw edges together and sew, using a ¼'' (6 mm) seam allowance. This seam is ⅛'' (3 mm) from the folded edge. Overcast the raw edges together. Press the seam allowance toward the blouse with the edge of the binding extending. Topstitch through all layers close to the seam. Sew the side seams.

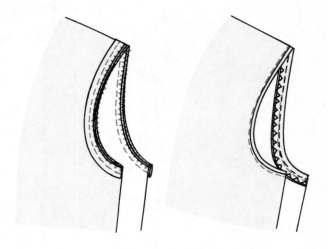

BUTTONS AND BUTTONHOLES

Buttonholes are placed on the right front and are horizontal or vertical. They are usually horizontal except when the blouse has a tab, then they are placed vertically in the middle of the tab. Buttonholes are usually from 3" (7.5 cm) to 4" (10 cm) apart. Horizontal buttonholes should be placed ⅛" (3 mm) from the center front. Vertical buttonholes should be placed along the center front. Sew on the buttons to match the buttonholes. For vertical buttonholes, sew on the buttons ⅛" (3 mm) down from the top of the buttonhole so that the blouse will hang evenly.

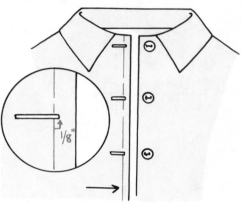

Make one or two buttonholes on the front part of each cuff (larger part of the sleeve). Sew on the buttons to match the buttonholes.

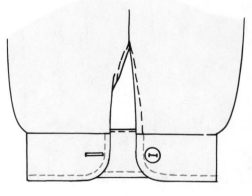

FAKE TAB

A tuck can make the front of a blouse look like it has a tab. The tuck is usually made on the right front but if you wish, you can make the tuck on both sides of the front.

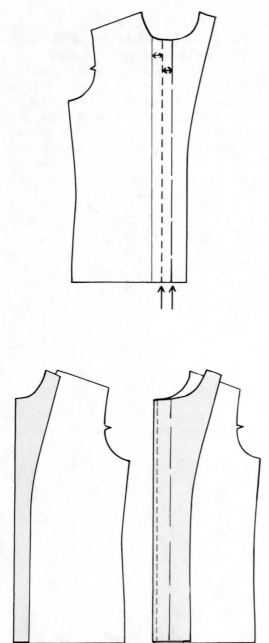

To allow for the tuck, measure the distance from the folding line to the center front. From this point, measure the same distance on the other side of the center front. Draw a line from the neck opening to the bottom edge. This line will be the line for the tuck. Cut the pattern apart on this line. Place a piece of paper under the pattern pieces. Spread the pattern apart ⅝'' (1.5 cm) which will be the allowance for the tuck. If you plan to have a tuck only on the right front, cut out the left front using the original pattern. Cut out the right front using the adjusted pattern.

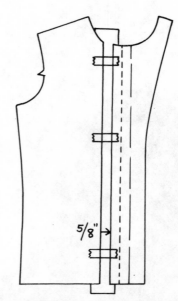

Fold the fronts on the folding line and press. On the right front, fold and press the line for the tuck. Sew a seam ¼'' (6 mm) from the pressed edge to form the tuck. Press the tuck towards the side of the blouse.

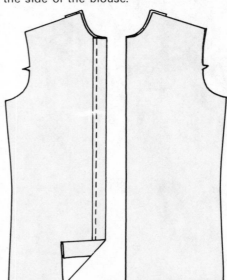

The rest of the construction is the same as previously described. After the blouse is completed, topstitch the outer edge of the front and the collar. Make vertical buttonholes in the middle of the tab. Sew on buttons to match the buttonholes.

TAB FRONT BLOUSE

A tab front blouse is very popular with either slacks or skirts. For a very attractive outfit, make the tab and the collar from the same fabric that you used for the slacks or the skirt and you have a matching ensemble. Even when you are using knit fabric for the blouse, you can make the tab from a woven fabric as long as the fabric is not too heavy.

The blouse may be constructed with or without interfacing. Interfacing tends to give the finished garment a more professional look. The easiest interfacing to use is the lightweight press-on interfacing.

For the tab, cut two pieces of interfacing from the folding line of the tab to the edges of the facing. You use interfacing only for the upper collar.

Place the interfacing on the wrong side of the upper collar and tabs. Press the interfacing to the fabric.

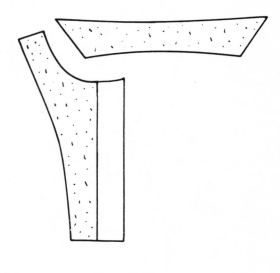

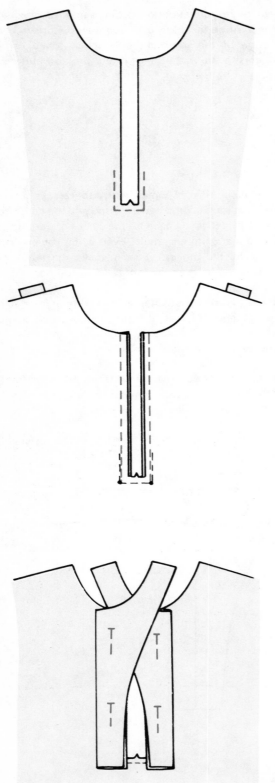

Press the tab front pieces on the folding line, wrong sides together.

On the bottom of the front opening, staystitch across the bottom and up 1'' (2.5 cm) on each side on the seam line.

Place the tabs on each side of the front opening, right side to right side, raw edges together and pin. The tab will extend ½'' (1.3 cm) below the opening.

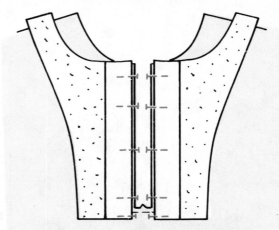

Begin sewing the seam at the neck opening using ¼'' (6 mm) seam allowance. Stop sewing ¼'' (6 mm) from the end of the tab (bottom of staystitching). Clip the seam allowance on the front to the corners of the staystitching.

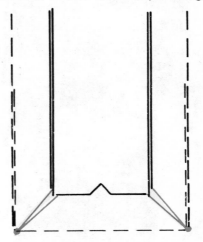

Turn the tab facing to the wrong side on the folding line. Pin in place.

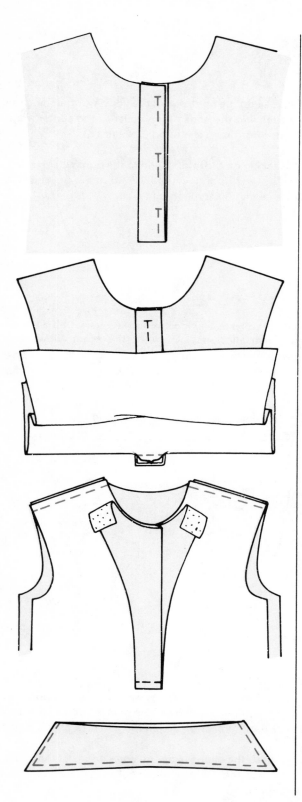

Overlap the right tab over the left tab, matching the neckline and the bottom edges. Pin together.

On the wrong side, secure the ends of the tabs to the front by sewing across the bottom edge of the tabs between the seams, following the staystitching line.

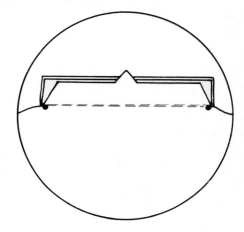

Sew the shoulder seams.

Place the collar pieces right sides together. Sew a seam on three sides, leaving the neckline open. Trim the corners. Turn right side out and make sure that the points of the collar are shaped correctly. Press the collar, favoring the upper collar edge, and roll the seam toward the under collar side. This will prevent the seam from showing from the right side.

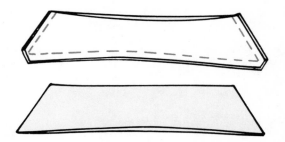

Topstitch the collar ¼'' (6 mm) from the edge.

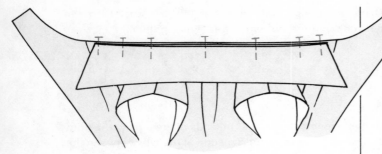

Pin the collar to the right side of the neckline, matching the center back and the ends of the collar to the center front. The center front is in the middle of the tab.

Fold the facing on the folding line to the right side over the collar. The facing will extend ¼'' (6 mm) beyond the shoulder seam. Pin through all layers.

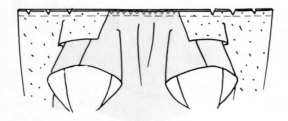

Sew on the collar by sewing through all layers. Clip the front **curved seam allowance. Overcast the seam allowances** together at the back neckline. Turn the facing to the inside and press. Attach the ends of the facing to the shoulder seams.

Finish the blouse as previously described.

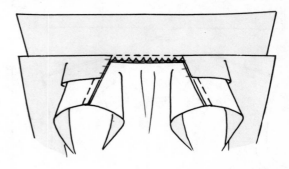

COLLAR STYLES

Collars on blouses change with fashion. One season they are wider, another narrower, more pointed or less pointed. It is very easy to change the shape and size of the collar.

Always make the changes on the outer edges of the collar. Never change the neckline of the collar as it will not fit the neck opening.

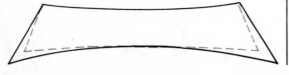

slacks
and
skirts

Slacks come in a great variety of styles, from very narrow legs to very full legs, which give the impression of wearing a skirt. Slack styles usually change from year to year and sometimes even from season to season. It is easy to adjust the leg styles to keep up with the current fashion.

When you choose a pattern, make sure you check which type of fabric for which the pattern is designed. If the pattern is designed for stretch fabric, it will not work very well for non-stretch fabric. A pattern designed for non-stretch fabric has more ease in the pattern and the crotch is designed in a different way.

When you buy a pattern for a pair of slacks, you use your hip measurement to determine your size. If you fall between two sizes, always choose the larger size as it is easier to decrease the pattern than it is to increase it.

It is very important to take your correct measurements. Refer to Section I. When you measure the length for slacks, be sure you wear the same style of shoes you plan to use when you wear the slacks. If you plan to wear high heels, the length should be longer than when you wear flat shoes.

The bottoms of slacks have various styles; Some may slant, others are cut straight across or they may have cuffs. Any adjustment for the length should be made at the knee area or on the line indicated on the pattern to shorten or lengthen the pattern.

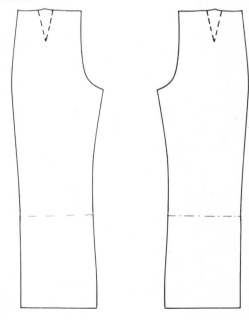

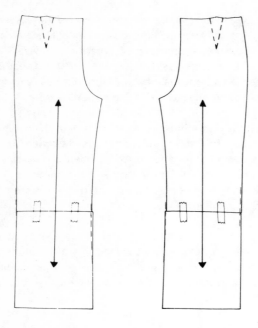

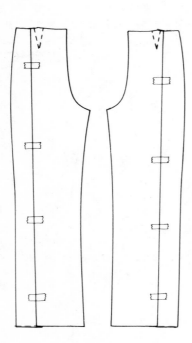

Cut the pattern apart at the point where you want to make the adjustment. To shorten the length, overlap the pattern and tape the pieces together.

To lengthen a pattern, place a piece of paper underneath, separate the pattern pieces as much as needed, and tape the pattern pieces to the piece of paper. Be sure to keep the grainline straight. To restore the leg design, draw a line over the adjusted area and cut off any excess paper.

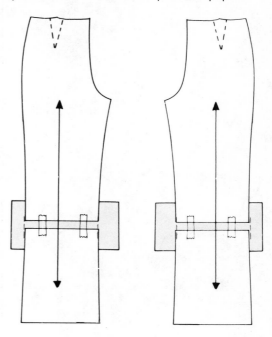

Compare your hip measurement with the pattern to determine if you have to increase or decrease the width of the pattern.

When measuring the pattern pieces, remember to allow for seam allowances. Also, allow for ease according to your personal preference. If the pattern has to be increased or decreased, use the following technique:

Draw a line on both the front and back pattern pieces from the middle of the waist down to the bottom of the slacks. Cut the pattern apart on this line. If the pattern calls for darts, do not draw the line through the darts. If you have to decrease the width, overlap the pattern the amount you wish to decrease the width.

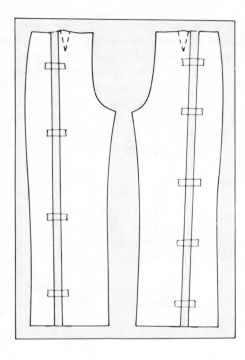

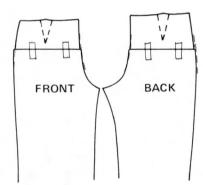

FRONT   BACK

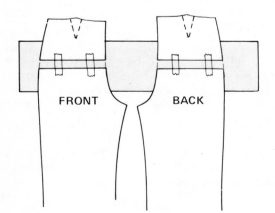

FRONT   BACK

If you wish to increase the width, place a strip of paper underneath the pattern, spread the pattern apart the necessary amount and tape in place. Restore the waist lines and the bottom of the pattern to their original shape.

If you are making a pair of slacks with a separate waistband, you should compare your crotch length with the pattern by drawing a horizontal line from the bottom of the crotch to the side seam on both the front and the back pattern pieces. At the center front, measure the distance from this line to the waist.

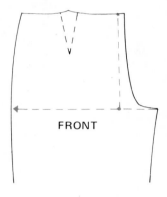

FRONT

If you have to shorten or lengthen the crotch length, draw a line halfway between the line at the crotch and the waist on both the front and back pattern pieces. Cut the pattern pieces apart at these lines. To shorten the crotch, overlap the pattern pieces the necessary amount and tape in place.

To lengthen the crotch, place a piece of paper underneath the pattern pieces, spread the pattern pieces apart the necessary amount and secure with tape. Restore the lines for the side seams and the lines for the center front and center back to their original shape.

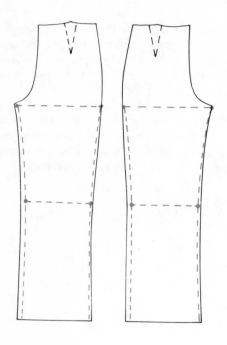

LEG CHANGES

If you have a favorite slacks pattern which fits you perfectly over your hips and at the crotch, but the style of the legs is not what you want, you can easily change the leg styles while leaving the rest of the pattern intact. You have to remember that any changes have to be made on both the inside and outside leg seams and on both the front and the back pattern pieces. Use the same procedure for both increasing and decreasing the width of the legs.

Draw a horizontal line on the pattern pieces at the knee and another horizontal line from the crotch to the outside leg seam. If you wish to decrease the width, you draw the lines inside the original pattern line. To increase the width, draw the line outside the original pattern line. Do not go above the crotch line as this will change the hip.

For any additional alterations refer to PROFESSIONAL **PATTERN ALTERATIONS MADE EASY**, published by KWIK·SEW Pattern Co., Inc.

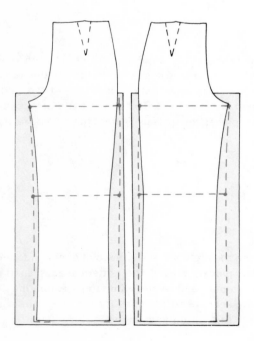

Slacks can be as simple or as complicated as you wish them to be. Using knit fabric you can eliminate both the zipper and a separate waistband. Because the fabric stretches you can get the slacks over your hips without a zipper and they still look attractive. However, if you prefer a more fitted pair of slacks, you should use a zipper and a separate waistband. The technique for sewing in the zipper is the same for both stretch and non-stretch fabric.

Before you cut out the fabric, place the fabric right side to right side. Be sure that you have the most stretch going around your body. When constructing slacks, it is extremely important that the grainlines on both layers of fabric are exactly straight. Now place the pattern pieces on the fabric following the grainline on the pattern. If you cut out the pattern and you do not follow the grainline, the legs will never hang straight. If you plan to have cuffs on the slacks, this should be taken into consideration.

Cut out the pattern. With the fabric right side to right side, start sewing the outside leg seam at the bottom of the leg and sew up to the waist. Press seam open.

Now, sew the inside leg seams again starting from the bottom of the slacks up to the crotch seam. It is very important that you start all the leg seams at the bottom and sew up the leg. If you do not do this, there is a possibility that one of the legs will twist.

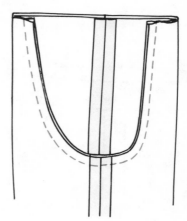

From this point on, construction is different depending upon how you wish to finish the waist.

PULL-ON SLACKS WITH FOLD-OVER CASING

Place one leg inside the other leg, right side to right side. Pin the crotch matching the inside leg seams and the waist. Sew the crotch seam starting from the center back all the way around to the front.

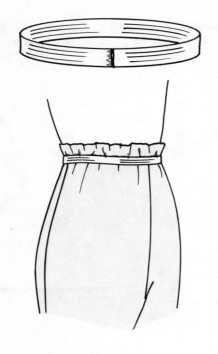

For the waist, we recommend a 1″ (2.5 cm) wide elastic. Cut the elastic the same length as your exact waist measurement plus the seam allowance. If the elastic is tighter than your exact measurement, the elastic will have a tendency to roll. How tight the elastic should be depends upon the type of elastic and how tight you want the waist. Overlap and sew the ends of the elastic together to form a circle.

To obtain the correct fit at the crotch, try on the slacks. Place the elastic over the slacks at your waist. Stand in front of a mirror and pull the slacks up until the crotch feels comfortable and the legs of the slacks hang straight. Mark with pins on the slacks at the top edge of the elastic. Remove the slacks and measure an additional 1¼″ (3.2 cm) up from the pins for the casing. Cut off the excess fabric at the top edge.

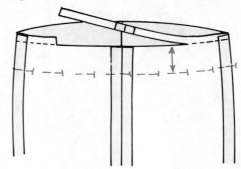

If the fabric has a tendency to unravel, overcast the top as well as the bottom of the slacks.

If you happen to have a narrow waist and you would prefer a snug fit, pin the seam at the center back and, if you wish, at the sides. Before you sew in these seams, make sure that the slacks slide easily over your hips.

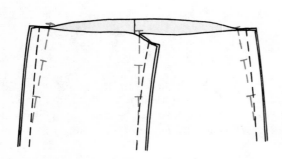

At the marked waistline, fold the fabric to the wrong side and press to form the casing.

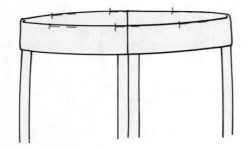

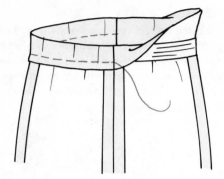

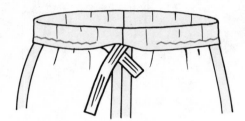

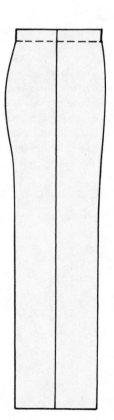

Place the elastic inside the casing and sew all the way around. Be careful that you do not sew through the elastic.

We suggest that when you sew this seam, you use a zipper presser foot. The best stitch to use is an elastic straight stitch or you can use a very small zigzag stitch. If you are using a regular straight stitch, be sure to stretch the fabric as you sew.

Another method is to sew the casing first, leaving a 1″ (2.5 cm) opening for threading the elastic. Pull the elastic through the opening and sew the ends together. Close the opening.

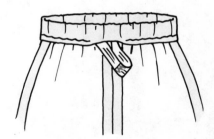

Hem the slacks at the desired length by folding the hem to the wrong side. Use a crisscross stitch. If your sewing machine has a blind stitch, you may prefer to use it for these hems.

Press the creases by lining up the inside and outside seams up to the knees. Above the knees, press the crease by following the grain line.

SEPARATE WAISTBAND

If you want to attach a separate waistband instead of using a casing in your slacks, the construction is the same up to the point where you mark the waistline. For a separate waistband, you mark the slacks at the bottom of the elastic, not at the top. Add ¼'' (6 mm) above the pins for the seam allowance. Cut off the excess fabric.

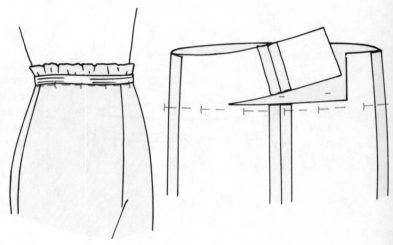

If you would prefer a snug fit, you can sew darts in the front and in the back. The darts should be placed in the middle as illustrated. Pin in the darts and try on the slacks to be certain that they are in the correct position. Be sure that the slacks slip easily over the hips. If you have an extremely narrow waistline and you would like the slacks to fit snugly, we suggest that you use a zipper. If you plan to use a zipper, follow the instructions in this section for fitted slacks.

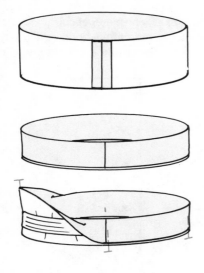

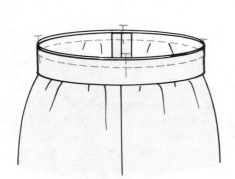

Cut a straight piece of fabric across the grain. The correct length is your waist measurement plus the seam allowance. This is for stretchy fabric. If you are using firm fabric, add to the length so that you will be sure it will go over your hips. If you are using 1'' (2.5 cm) wide elastic, the waistband should be 2⅝'' (6.8 cm) wide.

Sew the ends of the waistband together to form a circle. Press the seam open. Press the waistband double lengthwise, wrong sides together. Before sewing the waistband to the slacks be sure it slips easily over your hips.

Cut a 1'' (2.5 cm) width of elastic the length of your exact waist measurement. Sew the ends together to form a circle.

Pin the elastic close to the fold inside the waistband.

Divide the waistband opening and the waistband in fourths with pins.

Match the pins and sew the waistband to the slacks in one operation, right sides and raw edges together.

FAKE FLY

It is easy to add a fake fly on a pair of pull-on slacks. On the front pattern piece at the center front, add 1¼″ (3.2 cm) from the waist to the curve of the crotch. See illustration.

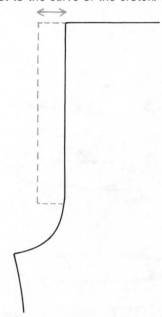

Pin the fronts together, right side to right side, and sew the front crotch curve. Lock the stitches at the extension and baste along the center front to the waist. Sew the outside edges of the extension from the waist to the bottom of the basting stitches. Press extension toward right front. On the right side, outline the fly by topstitching on the right front ⅞″ (2.2 cm) from the center front. Curve the seam at the bottom edge to the center front. Remove the center front basting.

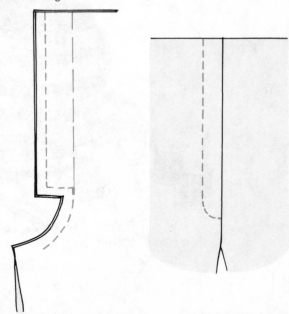

FITTED SLACKS

For a pair of fitted slacks which fit correctly, you should take your measurements and adjust the pattern as previously described.

Cut out the slacks being very careful to follow the grain line. Mark the dart positions on both the back and the front. Start by placing the fronts, right sides together. Sew the front crotch seam from point A to point B. Lock the stitches and baste along the center front from point B to the waist using long stitches. Clip the seam allowance at the end of the extension. Press the seam allowance open.

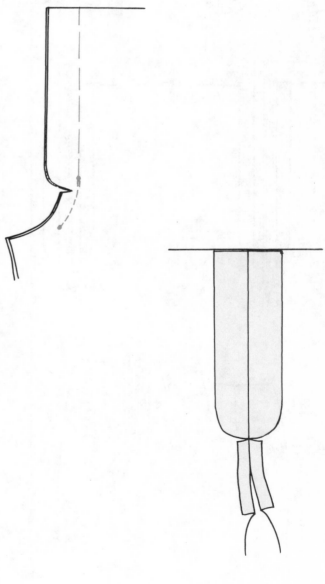

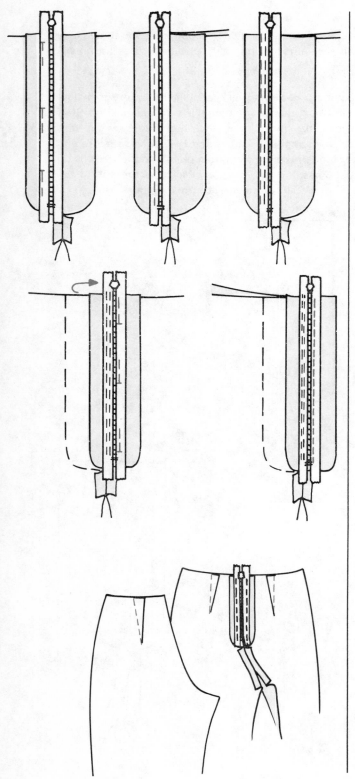

Place the closed zipper, right side down, on the front extension of the left front with the right edge of the zipper tape along the basted seam. The bottom of the zipper teeth should be ¼'' (6 mm) up from point B. The top of the zipper will extend up from the waist and should not be cut off until the waistband is sewn on.

Using a zipper foot, sew close to the zipper teeth through the zipper and the left fly extension. Sew again close to the edge of the zipper tape. Sew only through the zipper and the left fly extension.

Move the zipper toward the right fly extension as far as it will go without puckering underneath. You still have some seam allowance on the right side. Stitch close to the right side of the zipper teeth. Be sure to sew only through the zipper tape and the right fly extension. Press extension toward right front.

On the right side, outline the fly by topstitching on the right front 1'' (2.5 cm) from the center front. Curve the stitches at the bottom edge of the fly to the center front seam (point B). Remove the center front basting and open the zipper. If you prefer to have a zipper at the back or on a side, refer to Section VI for details on zipper insertion.

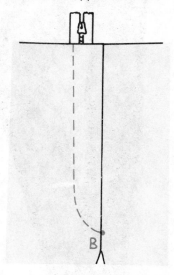

Sew all the darts in place. Press the darts towards the center.

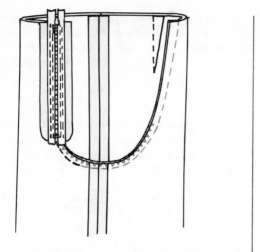

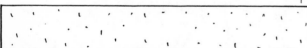

Sew the leg seams as previously described. Pin the center back seam, right sides together, matching the top edge of the waist and inside leg seams. Sew, starting from the top of the back waist and ending approximately 1″ (2.5 cm) over the front crotch seam. Trim the curved crotch seam allowance to ¼″ (6 mm). Overcast the raw edges together.

Press the interfacing to the wrong side of the waistband. Pin one edge of the waistband to the top edge of the slacks, right sides together, the left end of the waistband should extend ⅝″ (1.5 cm). The right end of the waistband should extend long enough to be used for the tab. Sew on the waistband. Cut off the excess length of the zipper so that it is even with the seam allowance. Press the seam allowance towards the waistband.

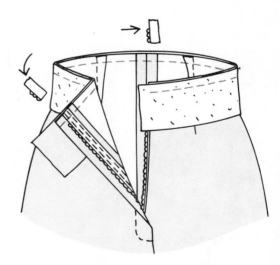

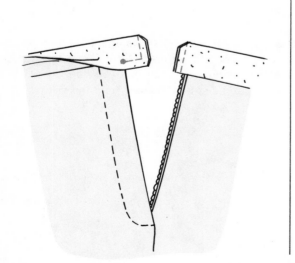

Fold each end of the waistband double, right sides and raw edges together. Sew across the end on the left front in line with the zipper teeth. On the right front, sew across the end and continue sewing to the center front. Grade the seam allowance and trim the corners. Turn right side out and press.

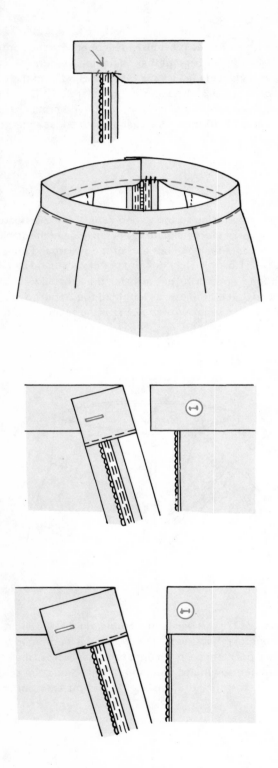

On the wrong side of the right end of the waistband, fold under the seam allowance and stitch by hand 1″ (2.5 cm) in from the tab. Now, on the right side, topstitch in the ditch the length of the waistband, with the raw edges of the waistband extending down beyond the seam.

Or, you can fold under the raw edges of the waistband. Be sure to cover the stitches. On the right side, stitch in the ditch. Be sure to catch the folded edge of the waistband with your stitches.

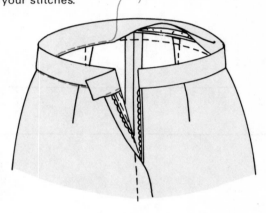

The tab can also be placed on the left front. The right front of the waistband will be even with the front of the pants. In this case, reverse the procedure for the left and right front.

Make a horizontal buttonhole on the right end of the waistband. Sew on a button on the left end of the waistband to match the buttonhole. You can use hooks and eyes instead of button and buttonholes. Hem the slacks.

102

CUFFS

Cuffs come and go depending upon whether or not they are considered fashionable at a particular moment.

Mark the length of the slacks. Decide how wide you wish to have the cuff. To the hemline, add twice the width of the cuff plus 1″ (2.5 cm). Example: If a 2″ (5 cm) cuff is desired, you would need an additional 5″ (13 cm) length from the hemline. Measure down the hemline the width of the desired cuff.

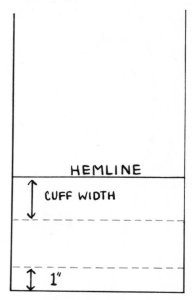

Fold the rest of the fabric to the wrong side and press. Now hem the slacks. Fold up the cuff at the hemline and press the cuff. Secure the cuff to the slacks by sewing a couple of stitches at the inside and outside leg seams.

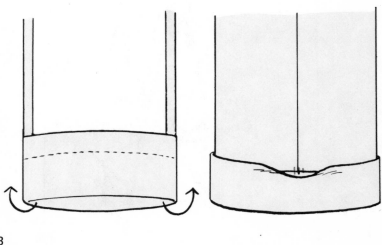

If you would like to add cuffs to the slacks and you do not have a long enough piece of fabric, you can sometimes make them by using fabric which would normally be discarded. If this is the case, leave a ¼'' (6 mm) seam allowance at the bottom of the slacks. To make separate cuffs, cut a piece of fabric long enough to go around the bottom of the slacks plus allowing for the seam allowance and twice as wide as you want the cuff to be. Sew the ends of the cuffs together to form circles which will exactly fit the bottom of the slacks.

Press the cuffs double lengthwise, with the wrong sides together. Sew the cuffs to the bottom of the slacks by placing the cuffs on the wrong side, raw edges together. Turn up the cuffs and press them. Secure the cuffs with a few hand stitches on the outside and inside leg seams.

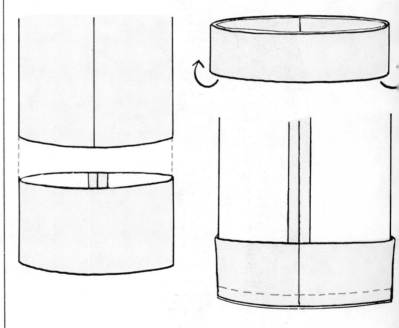

BELT LOOPS

If you prefer to have a belt with your slacks, we suggest that you use a slacks pattern which calls for a separate waistband.

First, decide how many belt loops you want to have and how wide you want them. The width and number depends upon personal preference. Rather than cutting a separate piece of fabric for each loop, it is easier to cut one long strip.

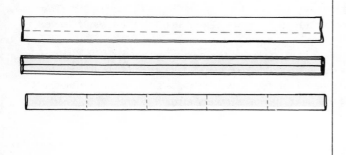

Sew the long edge. Press the seam allowance open. The seam should be in the middle of the strip. Turn the strip right side out. Now, cut off the loops at the desired length. Mark the slacks where you plan to attach the belt loops. The belt loops should be attached before you sew on the waistband. The most common number of belt loops for ladies' slacks is five. One edge of each loop should be overcasted. Pin the raw edge of the belt loops to the top edge of the slacks with the right sides together and with the seam on the belt loop facing up. Pin two loops to the front at the position of the darts; one at the center back and one on each side of the center back an equal distance from the center back and the front darts. Sew on the belt loops at the same time you sew on the waistband. Pin the other end of the belt loops to the waistband. Fold under the raw edges and sew across each loop close to the edge.

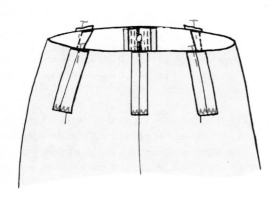

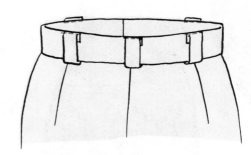

If you wish the loops to be longer than the width of the waistband, completely finish the slacks and attach the loops after the slacks are finished. Mark where the loops should be so that they are all an equal distance from the top of the waistband. Place the loops, right side to right side facing down. Sew across the width of the loop.

Fold the loops up to the correct position; fold under the seam allowance, edge to edge with the top of the slacks and sew across.

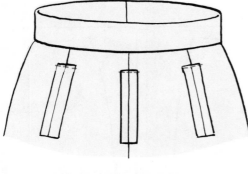

Permanent creases can be obtained by first pressing the slacks in the correct manner as previously described. Use an elastic straight stitch and sew a seam very close to the pressed crease. This can be done on both the back and the front but it is more common to do it only on the front crease.

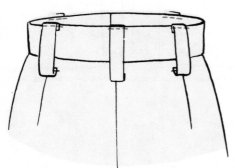

Another way to get the creases to stay is to press the slacks with a cloth which has been dampened with a solution of one-fourth cup of white vinegar diluted with two cups of water.

SKIRTS

Almost any type of fabric may be used for a skirt. The construction at the waist depends upon the type of fabric.

A simple skirt is one of the easiest garments to construct and the easiest skirt to construct is one made from sweater fabric or velour. If you use the same color fabric for the top and the skirt, it makes a very attractive ensemble.

Because of the stretch factor in the fabric, it is not necessary to have a separate waistband, zipper or darts. This is an excellent first garment for a new sewer to try.

If the fabric has no stretch or a small amount of stretch, it is necessary to use a zipper so that the skirt will slide easily over your hips.

Before cutting, check your hip measurement and the correct length of the skirt. Fold the fabric double, right side to right side, so that the edges are in the middle and you have a fold on each side. Place the center front and the center back of the pattern on a fold. Be sure that the greatest degree of stretch goes around the body.

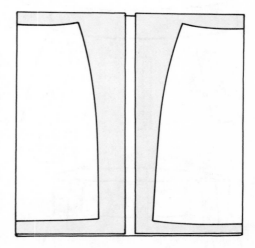

If you are using darts, start by sewing the front and back darts in place as these are easier to sew before you sew the side seams. Press the darts towards the center. Sew the side seams.

Decide how you wish to finish the waist. Refer to the construction of the waist given for slacks as they are the same except for the zipper insertion. See Section VI for zipper insertion.

A skirt can be very simple or it can be finished in a variety of ways all of which are very attractive. You can have a skirt with a slit, pleats, gores, vent, etc.

GORED SKIRTS

A gored skirt looks very attractive and is not as difficult to construct as some people imagine. The most common style uses four, six or ten gores. Decide how many gores you want and cut out all the gores in the same size. It is very important that you follow the grainline when you cut out the gores.

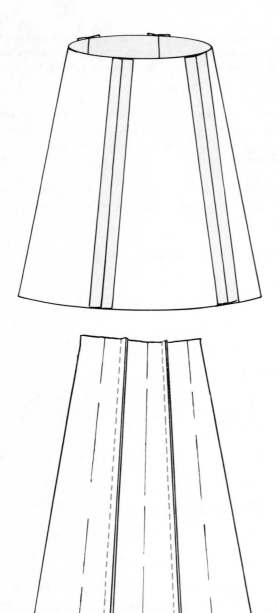

When you are using four or six gores, you sew the gores together with a wide enough seam allowance so that you can press the seam open.

Fold the hem to the wrong side and hem either by hand or by machine.

TEN GORES

Cut out the ten gores exactly the same size. Fold each gore lengthwise, wrong side to wrong side, and press a crease in the center of each gore.

Sew all the gore seams using ¼" (6 mm) seam allowance. Start sewing from the waist and stop at the hemline or 1½" (3.8 cm) from the bottom edge. Do not press the seams open.

Hem each gore separately; 1½" (3.8 cm) from the bottom.

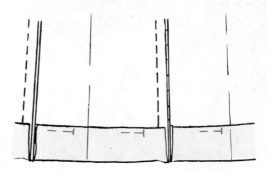

At the bottom of each seam, secure the hem to the skirt by sewing in the previous seam. Sew the width of the hem. At the bottom of each seam, fold in the seam allowances at an angle and sew together with a few stitches by hand.

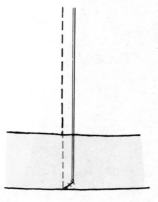

Fold each gore, wrong sides together, along the creased line. Topstitch on the right side very close to the edge along the crease line in the center of each gore.

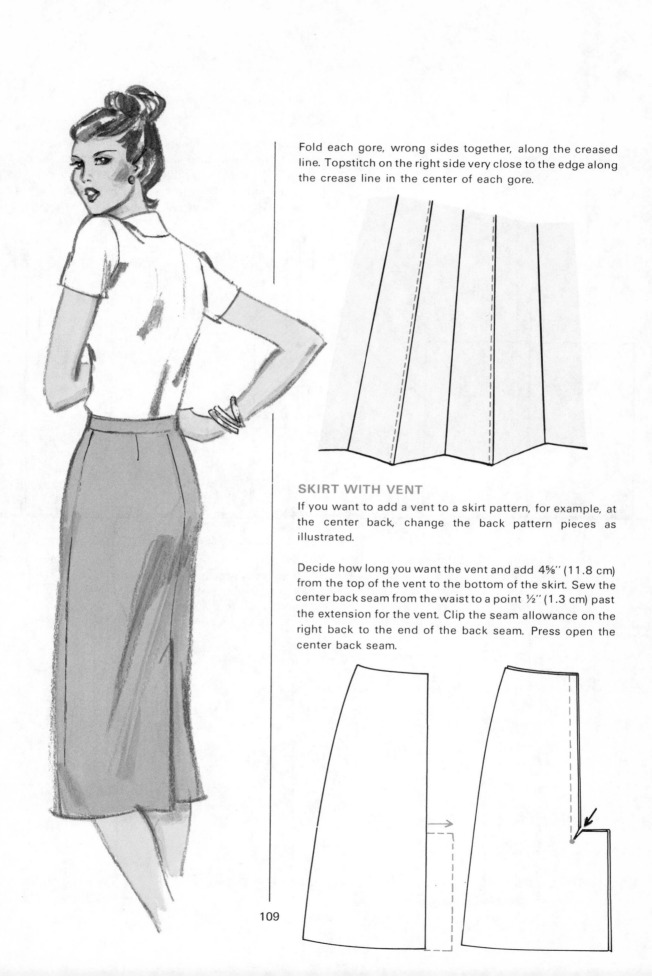

SKIRT WITH VENT

If you want to add a vent to a skirt pattern, for example, at the center back, change the back pattern pieces as illustrated.

Decide how long you want the vent and add 4⅝'' (11.8 cm) from the top of the vent to the bottom of the skirt. Sew the center back seam from the waist to a point ½'' (1.3 cm) past the extension for the vent. Clip the seam allowance on the right back to the end of the back seam. Press open the center back seam.

On the left back of the skirt as worn, fold the vent facing along the center back seam to the wrong side and press. On the right back, fold the extension 2⅝" (6.5 cm) from the edge, wrong sides together, and press. Trim the extension of the left back even with the folded extension of the right back. Overcast the raw edges of the extensions.

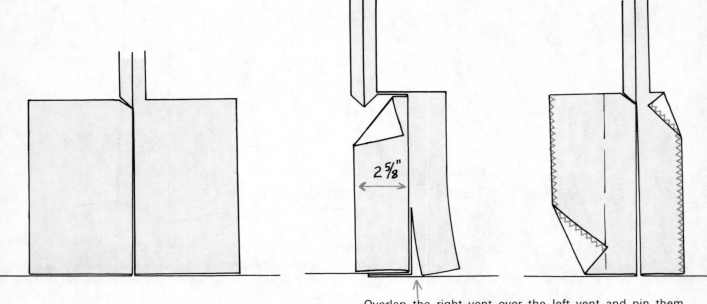

Overlap the right vent over the left vent and pin them together at the top edge to hold them in place. Topstitch across the vent at an angle, sewing from the center back to the edge of the vent through all layers. Trim the top of the vent close to the stitches.

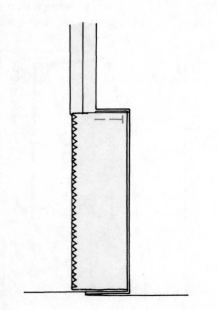

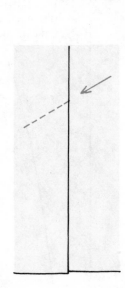

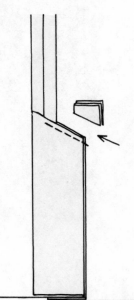

Finish the bottom edge of the back vent. Fold the vent facing on the folding line to the right side. Sew across the width of the facing 2″ (5 cm) from the bottom edge (hemline). Trim the hem on the facing. Turn the vent facing to the inside. Repeat for the other side of the vent.

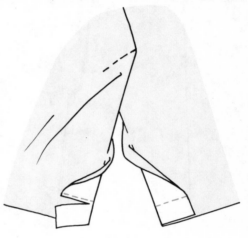

HEMLINE SLITS

A slit can be added to the skirt wherever there is a seam; at the center front, center back or the side seams.

Decide how long you want the slit and mark the top of the slit on the pattern piece. On the front and the back of the pattern pieces, add 1½″ (3.8 cm) from the seamline for the facing. Add this facing from the top of the slit to the bottom edge of the skirt. Cut the top of the facing at an angle as illustrated.

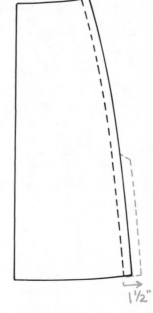

1½″

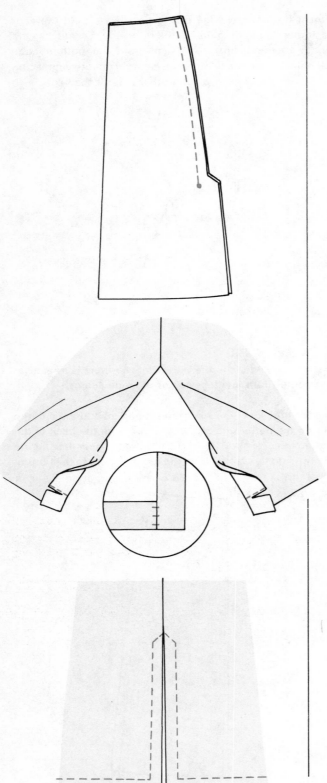

Start sewing ½" (1.3 cm) below the extension for the facing and sew to the waist. Press the seam and the extension open.

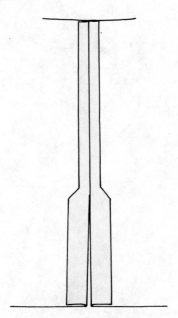

Finish the bottom edge of the slit by folding the facing to the right side and sew across the facing at the hemline. Trim the hem on the facing. Turn the facing to the inside. Hem the skirt. Attach the facing to the hem.

If desired, the slit can be topstitched and you can continue the topstitching around the hem.

112

zippers, yarn decorations and helpful hints

A zipper can be very practical and at the same time decorative. This is especially true if you are using a charm or a ring as a pull for the zipper. Some of the newer style zippers have wide tapes with very attractive designs. When using this type of zipper, the tape should be exposed. A zipper is very practical for a T-shirt, pull-over sweater, in addition to being very necessary for many dress styles. A zipper makes it much easier to put on and remove the garment without disturbing your hair.

If you are using a zipper and it is too long, always cut it off from the bottom. You can loosen the clamp on the bottom stop. Place the stop where you want it and tighten the clamp. Now cut off the excess zipper. If you have a zipper that sticks, run a little wax on the teeth. You will be amazed how much this will help, especially when used on heavy metal zippers.

The following methods for inserting zippers can be used in all types of fabrics.

EXPOSED ZIPPER

A short exposed zipper can be very attractive when used at the neck opening in front; it is very practical when used in a T-shirt or sweater at the back. Place the zipper along the center back or the center front and mark the length of the zipper with a pin. Cut a slit, stopping ¼″ (6 mm) from the pin.

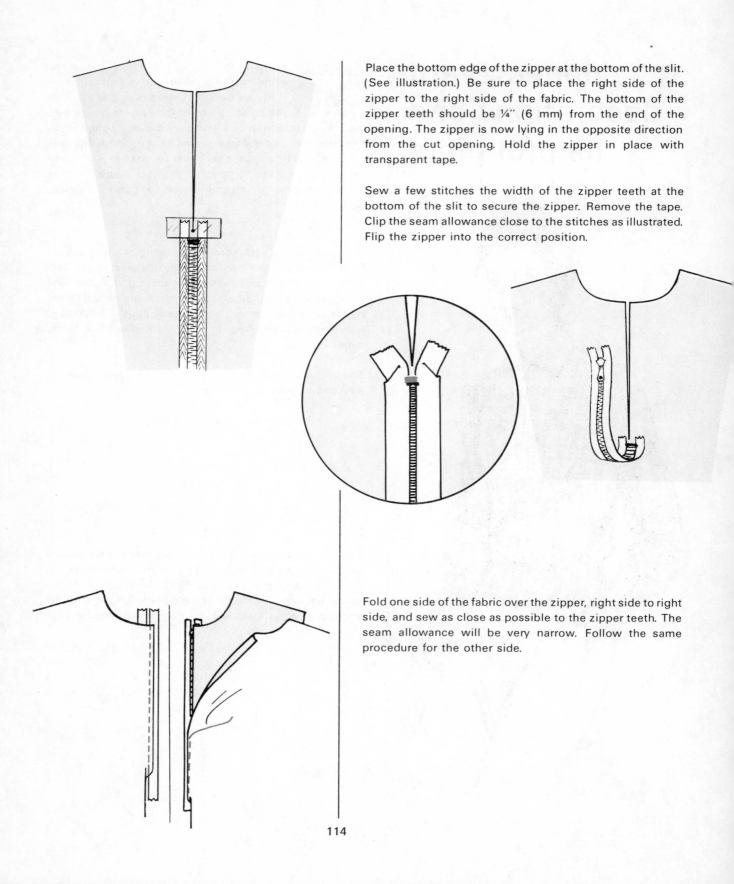

Place the bottom edge of the zipper at the bottom of the slit. (See illustration.) Be sure to place the right side of the zipper to the right side of the fabric. The bottom of the zipper teeth should be ¼" (6 mm) from the end of the opening. The zipper is now lying in the opposite direction from the cut opening. Hold the zipper in place with transparent tape.

Sew a few stitches the width of the zipper teeth at the bottom of the slit to secure the zipper. Remove the tape. Clip the seam allowance close to the stitches as illustrated. Flip the zipper into the correct position.

Fold one side of the fabric over the zipper, right side to right side, and sew as close as possible to the zipper teeth. The seam allowance will be very narrow. Follow the same procedure for the other side.

114

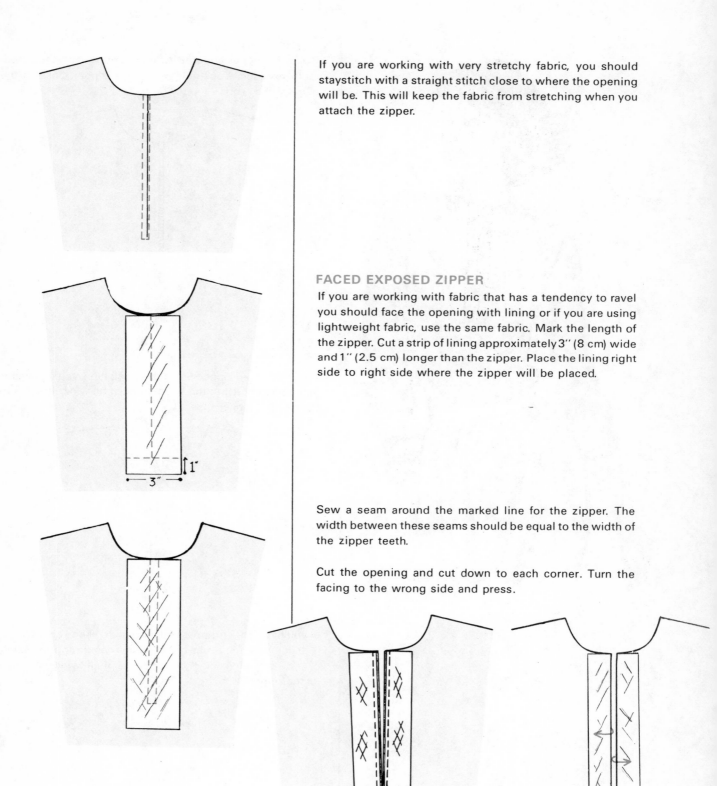

If you are working with very stretchy fabric, you should staystitch with a straight stitch close to where the opening will be. This will keep the fabric from stretching when you attach the zipper.

FACED EXPOSED ZIPPER

If you are working with fabric that has a tendency to ravel you should face the opening with lining or if you are using lightweight fabric, use the same fabric. Mark the length of the zipper. Cut a strip of lining approximately 3″ (8 cm) wide and 1″ (2.5 cm) longer than the zipper. Place the lining right side to right side where the zipper will be placed.

Sew a seam around the marked line for the zipper. The width between these seams should be equal to the width of the zipper teeth.

Cut the opening and cut down to each corner. Turn the facing to the wrong side and press.

Place the zipper underneath the opening with the zipper teeth exposed. Topstitch around the zipper close to the edge of the fabric.

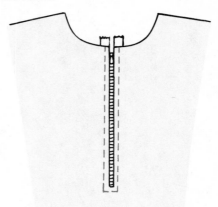

DECORATIVE ZIPPERS

For an exposed zipper with a designed tape, you follow the same procedure but the opening must be wider in order to expose the zipper tape.

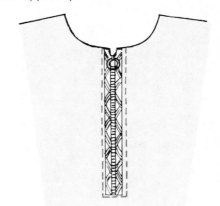

If you have a plain zipper and you would like to convert it to a decorative zipper, use a band with a design approximately ½" (1.3 cm) wide and 3" (8 cm) longer than twice the length of the zipper.

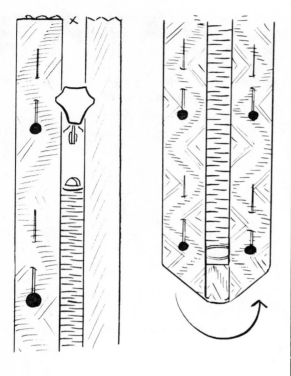

Place the band close to the zipper teeth on the right side edge to edge with the top of the zipper tape. Pin the band in place. At the bottom of the zipper, fold under the band to form a point. Continue pinning the band close to the teeth on the other side.

Sew on the band close to the teeth all the way around.

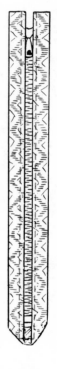

Mark the fabric where the zipper will be placed the exact length of the zipper teeth. Staystitch on both sides of this line. There should be a space approximately ¾″ (2 cm) between the staystitches.

3/4″

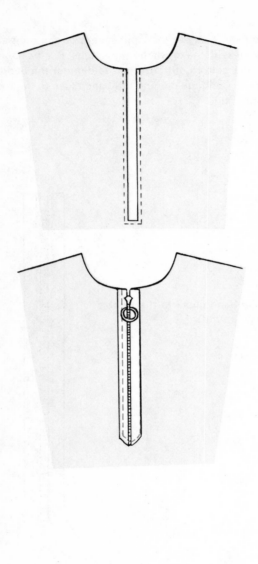

Cut away the fabric between the staystitches approximately ⅛″ (3 mm) away from the staystitches. If needed, overcast the raw edges.

Center the zipper over the opening. Sew on the zipper close to the outer edge of the zipper tape.

A simple method of applying a zipper with a designed tape is to place the zipper on the right side of the fabric, fold under the bottom tabs. Topstitch close to the outer edge of the zipper tape. Cut away the fabric underneath. If the fabric has a tendency to ravel, overcast the raw edges.

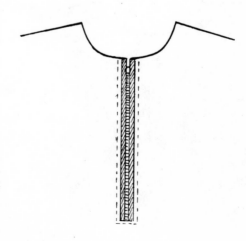

118

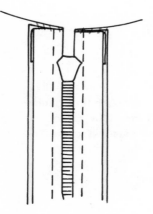

SEPARATING ZIPPER

A full length zipper should always separate at the bottom. Place the zipper on the center front with the rights sides together. Sew a seam close to the zipper teeth.

Open the zipper and follow the same procedure for the other side of the center front.

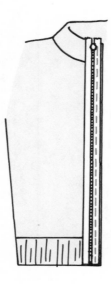

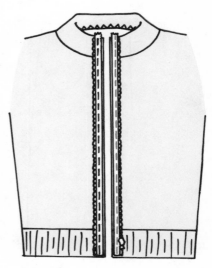

Turn the end tabs of the zipper under and finish with a few hand stitches.

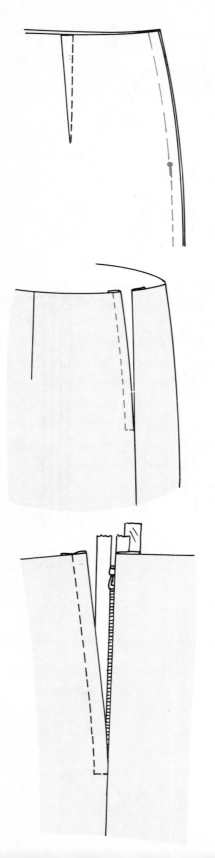

OVERLAP ZIPPER

This is also known as a hidden zipper and it is used wherever you have a seam and you would like to have a zipper which cannot be seen.

After you have sewn the seam to the point where you plan to insert the zipper, baste the zipper opening. This will make it easier for you to press the seam open evenly. After you have pressed the seam, remove the basting stitches.

Topstitch on the right side of the fabric ⅜" (1 cm) from the right side of the opening.

From this point on, you have to use a zipper foot on your sewing machine so that you can sew close to the teeth of the zipper.

Place a piece of transparent tape on the wrong side of the cloth edge of the zipper. About two-thirds of the tape should extend over the edge of the zipper tape.

Place the zipper underneath the opening with the edge of the teeth close to the fabric on the side of the opening which does not have the topstitching. The tape will hold the zipper in place.

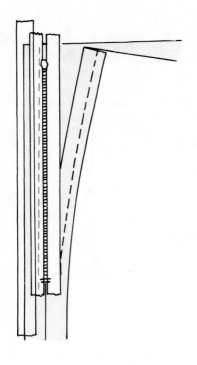

On the wrong side, sew on the zipper close to the zipper teeth.

Remove the tape. Now on the right side, place the other side over the zipper teeth and tape in place.

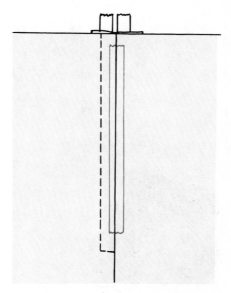

Now on the wrong side, sew a seam on the seam allowance as close as possible to the stitches. Remove the tape.

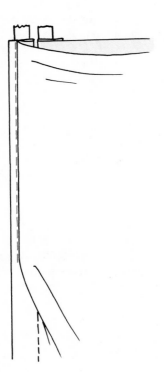

CENTERED ZIPPER

Baste the zipper opening together and press the seam open. Place the zipper underneath the opening with the teeth on the basted seam. Baste the zipper in place. On the right side, sew a seam starting at the top down to the end of the zipper across the bottom and up the other side. This seam should be ¼'' (6 mm) in from the zipper opening. Remove the basting stitches.

YARN DECORATION

You can very easily give a personal touch to any garment with the addition of yarn decorations or monograms. We recommend that you use the same type of yarn for the decoration that you used for the garment as different fibers react differently to heat and water. For example, on a wool sweater, use wool yarn for the decoration, on an Orlon sweater, use Orlon yarn.

MONOGRAM

A monogram or an emblem can easily be added to almost any garment. Many women prefer to place it on a pocket. If you intend to do this, remember to sew it onto the pocket before you sew the pocket to the garment. On almost all garments the most common location is the left front. Mark the monogram on the garment.

122

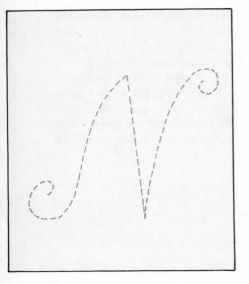

Use a piece of yarn in a contrasting color. Start at one end of an initial leaving a few inches of yarn at the beginning. Sew on the yarn using a zigzag stitch. This stitch should be wide enough so that it misses the yarn. Follow the outline of the initial, again leave a piece of extra yarn at the end.

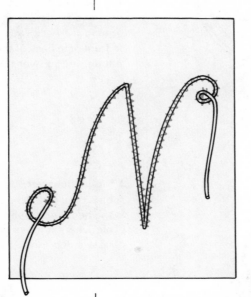

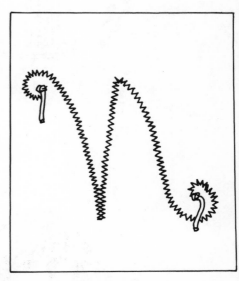

Pull the ends of the yarn to the wrong side and make a knot as close as possible to the fabric. The knots will keep the yarn in place.

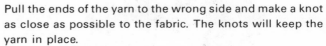

DECORATION

An extra touch to almost any garment can easily be made by the addition of a few strands of yarn. You can use this type of decoration around the cuffs, around the neck or straight up and down in the front. You can make the decoration in one solid color or you can use various colors. You can obtain a very interesting effect by taking a few different color yarns and twisting them together before you sew them on.

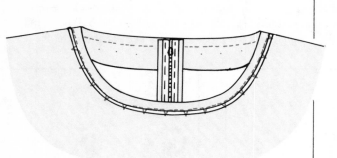

While you can use an ordinary zigzag stitch to sew on the yarn, you can obtain a much more attractive decoration by using a blind stitch. A blind stitch consists of a number of straight stitches then a large zigzag stitch. When using this stitch to sew on the yarn, the straight stitch goes close to the yarn but does not catch it. The zigzag stitch catches the yarn and holds it in place. If you are using yarn decoration around the neck, we suggest that you apply a zipper either in front or in back of the pullover as the yarn may not stretch enough to go over the head.

FRINGE

A fringe looks very difficult to make but actually it is quite simple. You can place a fringe decoration almost any place; at the hemline, around the sleeves or the neck, or any other place where it looks attractive. It is just as easy to make a double sided fringe as a single sided fringe.

DOUBLE SIDED FRINGE

A double sided fringe may be as wide or as narrow as you wish. The pattern illustrated is for a fringe 2½'' (6 cm) wide. Use hard cardboard for the pattern. If you would like to have a wider or narrower fringe, adjust the pattern accordingly. Wind the yarn closely around the pattern. The closer you wind the yarn, the thicker the fringe will be.

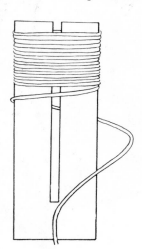

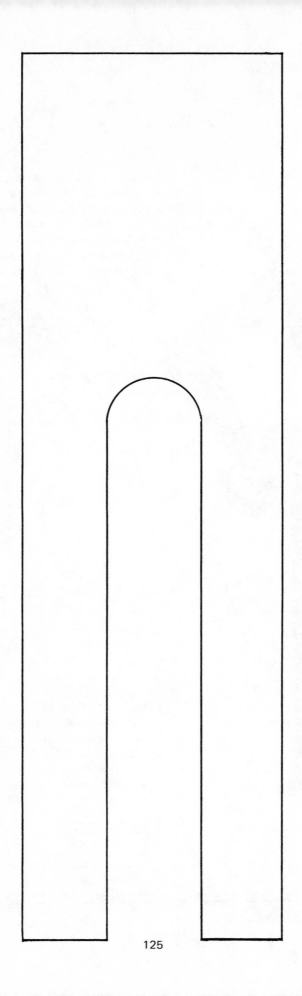

125

After you have wound the yarn on the pattern, place the pattern on the garment where you want to locate the fringe. The solid part of the pattern should be towards you. Sew a seam down the center moving the pattern towards you and winding on more yarn as you need it. You can leave the loops on the fringe or you can cut the loops. Both ways look very attractive.

SINGLE SIDED FRINGE

The easiest way to make a single sided fringe is to use a weaver's reed which is usually made of steel. As there is one narrow edge, cardboard is not stiff enough. If you wish to increase the width of the fringe and you are using a weaver's reed, you can do this by taping a piece of cardboard to the wide side. The rest of the technique is the same as you used for a double sided fringe.

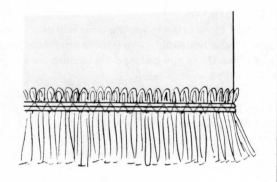

To give a more finished look to the garment, we suggest that you cover the stitches on the fringe by placing two strands of yarn over the row of stitches and sew them on with a zigzag stitch. You can use either the same color or a contrasting color.

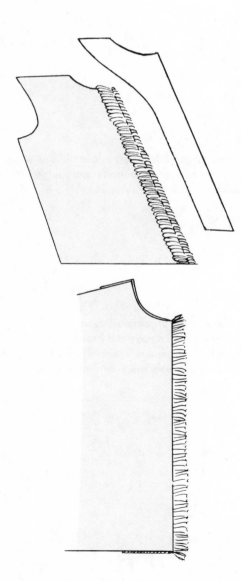

You can use a single fringe on the front edge of a jacket. Place the weaver's reed on the front edge of the jacket with the largest loops towards the side seam. Sew on the fringe as far as you wish to have it. Place the facing, right side to right side, on the front edge. Sew on the facing using a wide enough seam allowance to cover the stitches on the fringe. Turn the facing to the wrong side and press.

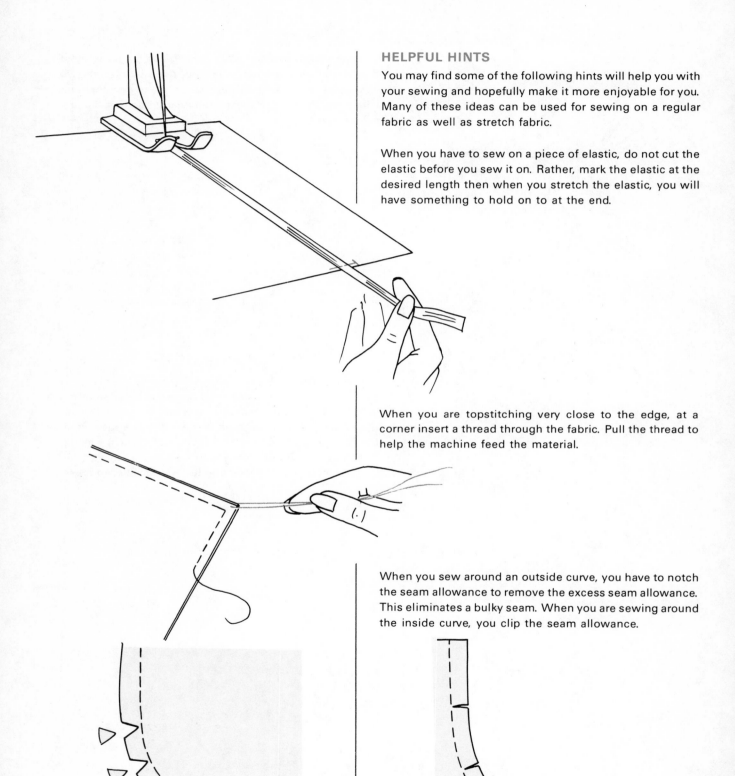

HELPFUL HINTS

You may find some of the following hints will help you with your sewing and hopefully make it more enjoyable for you. Many of these ideas can be used for sewing on a regular fabric as well as stretch fabric.

When you have to sew on a piece of elastic, do not cut the elastic before you sew it on. Rather, mark the elastic at the desired length then when you stretch the elastic, you will have something to hold on to at the end.

When you are topstitching very close to the edge, at a corner insert a thread through the fabric. Pull the thread to help the machine feed the material.

When you sew around an outside curve, you have to notch the seam allowance to remove the excess seam allowance. This eliminates a bulky seam. When you are sewing around the inside curve, you clip the seam allowance.

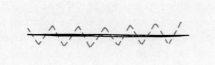

An easy way to repair a rip is to place a piece of press-on interfacing underneath the rip, force the edges of the rip together and press. Be sure not to use too large a piece of interfacing as is may stiffen the fabric. This will give you an almost invisible mend; for children's clothes, you may want to reinforce the mend with a three step zigzag stitch.

You can sometimes repair a small hole by taking a little of the same fabric, for instance from a seam allowance, and shredding the fabric with a pair of scissors. Place the shredded fabric on the press-on interfacing, place the garment on the interfacing with the hole over the shredded fabric and press.

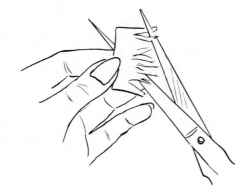

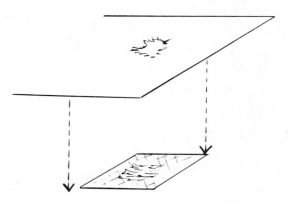

Never cut off the loops when you get a snag in a garment, this can cause a run or even a hole. Use a wire needle threader or a fine crochet hook to pull the thread or yarn to the wrong side.

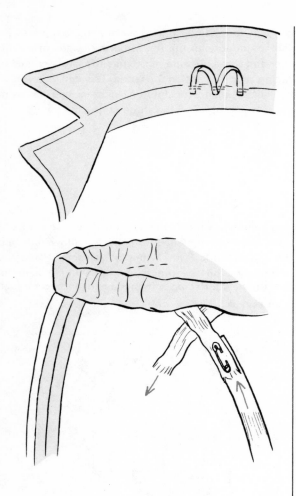

If you are using a loop at the top of children's garments so they can be hung on a hook, make them of elastic. Sew them at both ends and at the middle. If one seam breaks the garment can still be hung up.

To replace a worn elastic waistband, cut a piece of new elastic the correct length. Make a small opening in the waistband casing, pull out a loop of the old elastic and cut it. Using a safety pin, pin one of the ends of the replacement elastic to the old elastic and pull the new elastic in place. Sew the ends of the new elastic together.

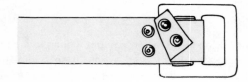

As some belt buckles are damaged in the laundry, use snaps or hooks to attach the buckle. Remove the buckle before cleaning the garment.

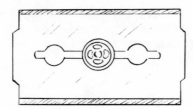

If you have to use a razor blade to rip apart a seam, it is easier to hold the razor blade if you place a large snap in the center of the blade. This also makes the blade a lot more rigid.

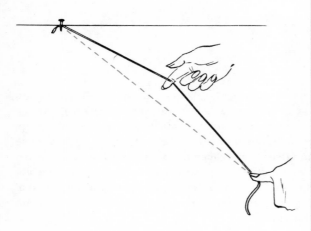

It is extremely difficult to cut a straight line or for that matter, to sew a perfectly straight seam when you have nothing to guide you but your eyes. When you are sewing a side seam or making pleats and it is important that you obtain a straight line, mark the line with chalk using the following procedure:

Take a piece of fine string or coarse thread, such as crochet thread, coat the thread or string with chalk. Tie one end around a pin or thumb tack and insert the pin or thumb tack at the point where you wish the line to begin. Hold the thread or string tightly where the seam will end. Snap the thread by lifting it at the middle and releasing it.

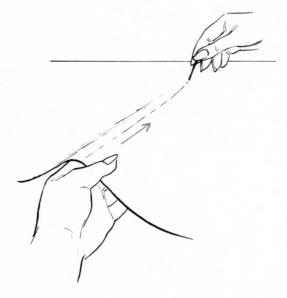

To obtain a straight line on non-stretch fabric, hold the fabric with one hand. Hold a pin in your other hand and starting at the point where you wish the line to begin, draw the pin rapidly across the fabric. The pin will follow the grain in the fabric and give you a perfectly straight line.

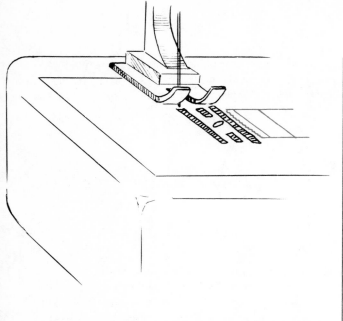

A simple method to get an even seam allowance is to place a piece of tape on the bed of your sewing machine. Mark on the tape the various seam allowances which you will be using.

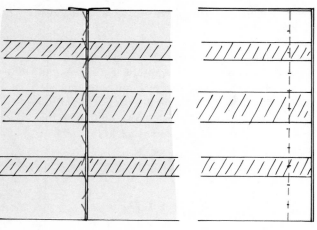

To obtain a perfectly matched seam when sewing on stripes, checks or plaids fold and press the seam allowance to the wrong side. Turn the fabric to the right side and using a narrow zigzag with a long stitch length and a very loose tension, baste the pieces together being careful to match the pattern on the two pieces of fabric. Turn the fabric to the wrong side, open the seam allowance and using a normal stitch length, sew the seam on the fold. Remove the zigzag basting stitches.

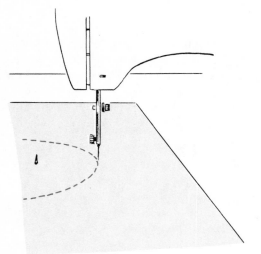

To sew a perfect circle, place a thumb tack on your sewing machine with the point sticking up. Hold the thumb tack in place with a piece of transparent tape. Poke the tack through the fabric and you pivot the fabric around the tack as you sew. You can obtain some beautiful decorations when you use decorative stitches also called machine embroidery.

An easy method for gathering is to zigzag over a strong thread such as buttonhole twist. Be sure not to catch the thread with the stitches. Pull the thread to gather the fabric as much as desired. After the garment has been completed, you can easily remove the thread.

It is very difficult to obtain an even hemline if you do not have anyone to assist you. Here is an easy way which you may want to try. Tape a chalked cord between a doorjam at the height you wish your skirt to be. Turn around slowly and the chalk will mark the hemline. Make a note of the distance from the floor to the cord and you will always be able to obtain hems the same length.

When you are making a hem and you are not sure of the correct length, use tape instead of pins to hold the hem in place. This will eliminate runs in your hose and save you from being stuck with the pins. This also applies when you are determining the length of sleeves.

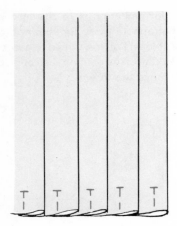

If you are traveling and have a pleated skirt, pin each pleat at the bottom. This will keep the pleats in much better condition when the skirt is packed.

Plastic is difficult to sew because it ripples and has a tendency to tear where the needle penetrates it. To overcome these problems, use a fine sewing machine needle and long straight stitches. Place a little oil on your finger and hold your finger in front of the needle as you sew.

A roller presser foot is often helpful when sewing on heavy plastic and vinyl.

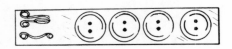

If your garment calls for a lot of small buttons, you can keep track of them by placing them on a piece of transparent tape. This way you always know where they are. This is also useful for snaps and hooks.

When you have finished sewing and you still have some thread left on the spool, use a small piece of tape to hold the end of the thread in place. You will be amazed how neat your sewing drawer will look.

swimsuits

Swimsuits have changed dramatically over the past fifty years. Compare the styles on a picture of a beach scene fifty years ago to what you observe today and you will be amazed at the difference.

Not only have the styles changed but modern technology has made possible an almost complete change in the material used for swimsuits. At one time wool was considered the only fabric to use. This was because it was considered to be warmer than cotton and also had more ability to "give" thus making it more comfortable. While this was important, wool had many disadvantages. What could be more uncomfortable than having to put back on a wool suit not completely dry, or what a shock to get out the wool swimsuit in the spring only to find a couple of large moth holes? Modern fabrics dry much quicker than wool as the fabric itself does not absorb moisture; the droplets of water are held between the threads of the fabric but are not absorbed by it.

Nylon plus spandex is probably the most popular fabric for swimsuits. However, you can find many other fabrics which are also used.

There are many variations for swimsuits. You may want to make several using different designs so that you can determine which design suits you best. All of them are relatively easy to construct and do not take much time. From any of the basic patterns you pick, you can create your own variations so that you can be certain that no one else at the beach will appear in the same suit as yours.

Stretch

There are many advantages to sewing your own swimsuits. Not only can you save money and thus be able to afford more than one, but you can now have swimsuits which fit you perfectly. Gone will be the rough red marks where perhaps the elastic in the leg opening dug into your body. When you construct your own suit you will have a suit fitted exactly for you.

When constructing a swimsuit, it is very important to use the correct pattern. This is especially true when you are using stretch fabric.

If you use a pattern for non-stretch fabric, and use stretch fabric, the result will be a garment which is much too large. When constructing a garment using non-stretch fabric and a pattern for stretch fabric is used, the swimsuit will be too small.

To be certain that you are obtaining the correct pattern size, check the sizes on the back of the pattern envelope and compare these with the actual body measurements, Also be sure to check what kind of fabric for which the pattern was designed. Swimsuit fabric can be two-way stretch, one-way stretch or no stretch.

On the back of the pattern envelope there is a stretch chart. Before you buy the fabric, check to make sure that the stretch of the fabric corresponds with the pattern as there is a great difference in the amount of stretch in various fabrics.

When you are using stretch fabric, the greatest amount of stretch always goes around the body. It is also important to choose the correct notions as both salt and chlorine not only bleach but also tend to deteriorate elastic, bra cups, etc.

There is a special elastic treated to retain its elasticity when exposed to chlorine or salt water. If you use regular elastic, there is the chance that you will end up with the bottom of a two-piece suit sliding down. Almost all swimsuit patterns call for elastic ⅜" 1 (cm) wide except for men's and boys' trunks which call for a wider elastic around the waist. This special elastic can be obtained in most of the fabric stores which carry swimsuit fabric.

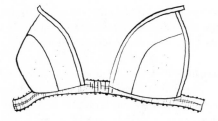

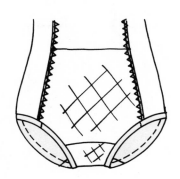

The most common type of swimsuit bra cups are molded and are usually made from polyester with lace or acetate lining. When using a cup with a lining, the lining should go toward your body. This is the opposite procedure to that used when making a regular bra. When constructing a regular bra you always show the pretty side out. The easiest type of bra cups to use when constructing a swimsuit is the type which has a piece of elastic at the bottom. The elastic should extend at each side to be sewn on to the side seam of the suit.

It is not necessary to line the entire swimsuit. We do suggest, however, to line the crotch and part of the center front.

If the fabric is lightweight, it may be necessary to line the entire swimsuit. The most suitable lining is made from two-way stretch banlon or nylon.

You can construct a swimsuit on any kind of sewing machine using any type of stitch but naturally some stitches are more suitable than others as the seam must be strong enough to hold when the swimsuit is stretched. The best stitches for making this kind of garment are found on the more sophisticated sewing machines which have reverse cycles.

When using a reverse cycle machine the best stitch to use is the overlock stitch which sews the seam and overcasts in one operation. This is a stretch stitch so you do not have to stretch the fabric while sewing. This stitch saves you a great amount of time as you do not have to sew the seam twice.

For a regular zigzag machine, set the stitch length at medium and the width at slightly less than medium, Stretch the fabric slightly while sewing.

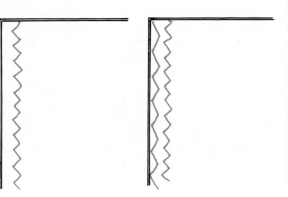

As swimwear fabric seldom requires overcasting to prevent raveling, it is not necessary to overcast the edges. But to obtain a stronger seam, we recommend that you overcast the edges together using the largest zigzag stitch on your machine.

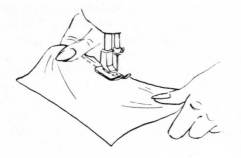

If you are using a plain straight stitch machine, you can still make a satisfactory seam by stretching the fabric in back as well as in front of the presser foot while sewing.

Sew the seam two or three times close together, using a medium stitch length. In order to avoid a possible embarrassing moment, perhaps even longer than a moment, we strongly suggest that you overcast the seam by hand. This hand overcasting is called "seam insurance".

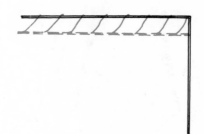

If your sewing machine has a tendency to skip stitches, this is usually caused by a dull or bent needle. This may not show when sewing on a non-stretch type of fabric. The most important rule to follow when sewing swimwear fabric is to use a fine and sharp needle, size 10 or 11. You should always bear in mind that swimsuit fabric is a very tough fabric and it has a tendency to dull the needle. Even though you may start out with a new sharp needle, you will find that you have to change the needle more often than when sewing with natural fabrics.

If after changing the needle, the machine still skips stitches, you can often correct this by increasing the pressure on the presser foot as the skipped stitches are usually caused by the fabric following the needle down the needle hole, causing a reduction in the size of the bottom loop. As a result the hook misses the loop.

If the fabric you are using contains spandex and you have to press with an iron, set the iron for a low temperature setting. Move the iron rapidly and do not leave it in one position very long. Actually, when you are constructing a swimsuit, no ironing, or very little, is necessary as the fabric will stretch out when you put on the suit.

As there are so many different styles for swimsuits, we will only cover a few basic styles. The technique for sewing swimsuits is the same regardless of the style.

ONE PIECE SWIMSUIT

Before you start cutting, place the fabric double, right side to right side. Make sure the fold is along the grain in order to insure a proper fit and that the greatest degree of stretch goes around the body. Cut out the pattern pieces.

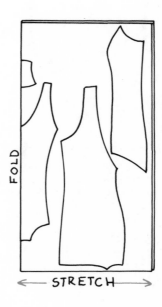

As it is often difficult to tell one piece from another as you cut out the pieces, mark each piece using a piece of transparent tape. If you plan to line part or the entire swimsuit, the lining should be cut out at this time.

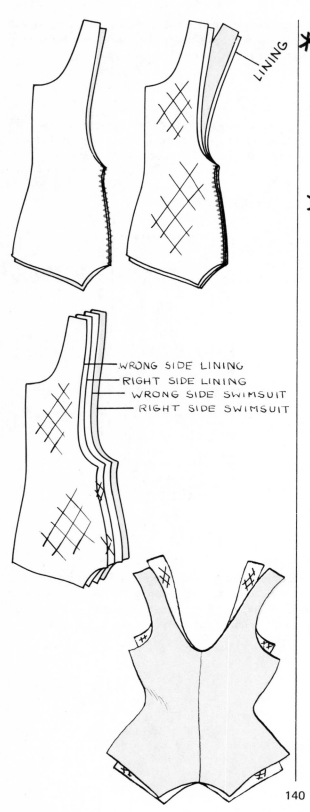

The first seam to sew is the center back. If you plan to line the entire swimsuit, sew the lining at the same time as you sew the swimsuit fabric. Place the swimsuit fabric between the lining. You now sew through four layers.

Or you can sew the lining separately and the swimsuit separately and join them together at the arm, leg and neck openings. We do not recommend this technique as the seams in the lining have a tendency to show through.

Another method of sewing the lining which gives you hidden seams in front and in the back but not at the side seams, is to place the swimsuit fabric right side to right side and the lining right side to right side on top of each other, with the lining on top of the swimsuit fabric. Sew the seam through all four layers.

Open up the lining and the lining will cover up the seam.

140

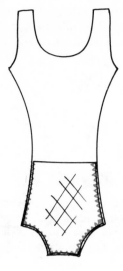

It is not necessary to line the entire swimsuit. We do suggest, however, to line the crotch and part of the center front.

If you plan to line the bottom of the front panel, place the lining on the swimsuit fabric, wrong sides together. Sew a seam close to the edge all the way around but not across the top. This makes it easier to handle the rest of the seams and it will assure you that the lining will lie flat.

Now sew the two front side seams together. Be sure to match the notches so that you will be assured of obtaining the correct curve over the bust.

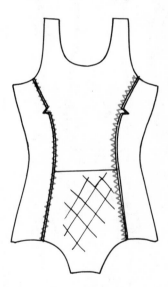

Place the front of the crotch piece, right side to right side to the front of the swimsuit. Place the front of the crotch lining right side to right side. Sew the seam through all four layers.

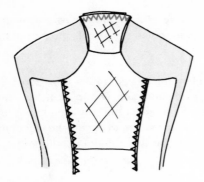

Now sew the back of the crotch to the back of the swimsuit, as the crotch piece curves less than the back piece, it is easier to have the crotch piece on top when sewing.

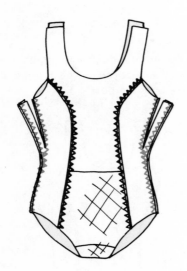

AFTER CLOSING SIDE SEAMS

Place the back and the front of the swimsuit, right side to right side, and sew the side seams. Try on the suit. If you believe that the suit is too loose or if the bust line is too large, this can easily be changed by sewing a seam inside any seam and cut off the excess.

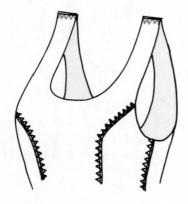

Sew the shoulder seams together, place the fabric right side to right side and sew across.

The leg, arm and decolletage openings are finished off by using ⅜'' (1 cm) swimsuit elastic.

Normally the pattern indicates the length of elastic you need.

As the thickness of everyone's arms and legs vary, the best method of determining how long the elastic should be is to measure the exact amount of elastic needed.

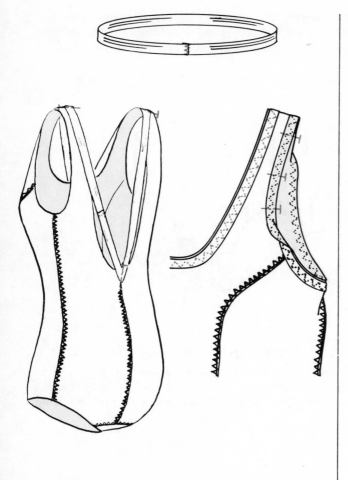

Sew all five strips of elastic by overlapping the ends ¼" (6 mm) to form circles.

To apply the elastic, place the elastic on the wrong side of the fabric, elastic edge to the cut edge. Sew on the elastic by stretching the elastic both in back as well as in front of the presser foot as you sew. The best stitch to use is the three-step zigzag stitch. This stitch has three small stitches in each zig and in each zag.

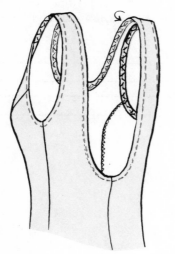

If your machine does not have a three-step zigzag stitch, you can use a large zigzag stitch. If you are using a straight stitch sewing machine set the stitch length at slightly longer than medium length. To finish the edge where the elastic is sewn, turn the elastic under to the wrong side and topstitch approximately ¼" (6 mm) in from the folded edge, being sure to catch the elastic on the wrong side. Again, you stretch the elastic while sewing.

When sewing the elastic on the leg openings, sew the elastic on the front of the suit without stretching the elastic. Stretch the elastic across the back to fit the opening.

If you are using the bra cups with the elastic tabs, now is the time to sew in the cups.

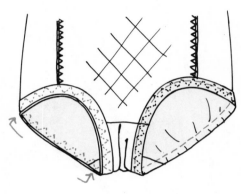

ADDING STRIPES TO A ONE-PIECE SWIMSUIT

If you are using a pattern with a princess line, it is very attractive to add a vertical stripe to the front side seams. These contrasting stripes will give a slimming effect to the suit.

For a ½'' (1.3 cm) finished stripe, cut two strips of contrasting fabric 1½'' (3.8 cm) wide and the length of the front.

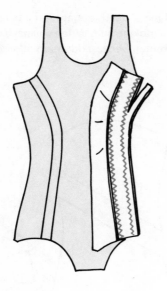

Pin the stripe to the front and side panel. Sew them together using a ½'' (1.3 cm) seam allowance. Trim the seams to ¼'' (6 mm).

If you are using a pattern with a one-piece front, you can add diagonal stripes. Mark the location of the stripe. Decide how wide you want the stripe. Cut out the stripe, adding ¼'' (6 mm) seam allowance on each side. Cut the pattern the width of the finished stripe minus the seam allowance. Cut out the fabric. Sew on the stripe. The rest of the construction is the same as previously described.

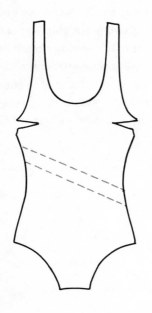

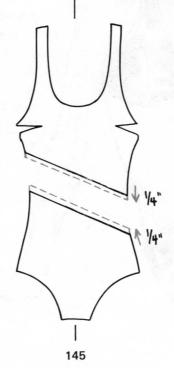

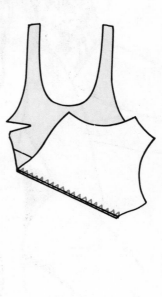

The same technique is used for geometric cuts which give you a very original looking suit. When you have cut apart the pattern, always remember to add seam allowances.

TWO-PIECE SWIMSUIT

The advantage of a two-piece swimsuit is that you are free to use a much larger selection of fabric than when constructing a one-piece suit. You always use two-way stretch fabric in a one piece suit, while for a two-piece suit, you can use either two-way stretch, one-way stretch or non-stretch fabric. Always remember that when using one-way stretch fabric, the stretch goes around the body. Two-piece swimsuits are preferred by many as they expose more area to the sun.

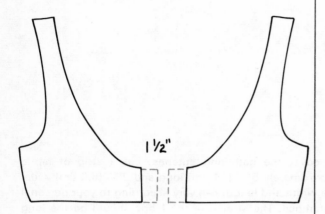

The techniques for making a two-piece swimsuit are the same as used for a one-piece swimsuit except that you have a separate top and bottom. There are many styles available.

Some of the patterns have tops which are pullover style but if you prefer to use a hook opening at the center back, add 1½″ (3.8 cm) at the center back to both sides.

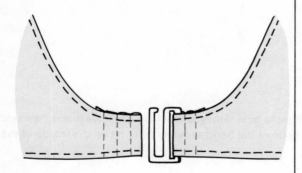

After you have applied the elastic, apply the hook. On the right side of the back, insert the end of the top through the hook, fold along the center back and sew in place. Sew close to the hook and then sew another seam close to the raw edges. On the left side of the back, fold the end of the back along the center back to the wrong side. Sew ⅜″ (1 cm) from the folded edge. Add another two rows of stitches so that the top can be adjusted.

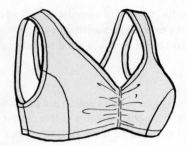

GATHERED FRONT WITH BAND

If you would like to obtain a gathered look at the center front, gather the front as much as desired.

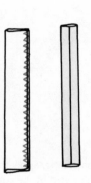

To cover the gathering stitches, cut a strip of fabric approximately 5½" (14 cm) long and 2½" (6.5 cm) wide. The width and length can vary according to your personal preference. The stretch of the fabric should go the long way. Fold the band double, right side to right side, lengthwise. Sew the long side. Turn the band right side out. Place the seam in the center of the band. The band goes around the center front.

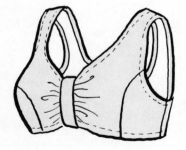

Determine how tight you would like to have it and then sew the ends of the band securely by hand on the inside of the top.